W C L D N

Glen Wilson

Contents

Introduction

I'll level with you from the off. I don't quite know what this is. It's too short to be a proper book, too long to be an article, too much about watching football to be a novella.

I've never been much of a salesman.

Anyway, in the summer of 2018, as someone long fascinated by London's remarkable multiculturalism, I decided to write about how the city watched the World Cup; about how such a concentrated global population digested one the most global of sports events.

But this isn't that. Not quite.

Because in the summer of 2018 I was also struggling. I was suffering with depression. Really suffering. To a point where I could no longer ignore it, wash over it, pretend that all was fine. Not inwardly anyway.

The result of these two facets is this. An observation of a long hot football summer in a remarkable city, but one sketched from a hole. One that I thought, and hoped, a month of football might haul me out of.

So, if this is anything, it's that. And I think writing it helped.

The build up

The anticipation

You had forgotten this was a World Cup year. But then you were largely oblivious to much that existed in the wider world. Not looking forwards, too often looking back. Just trying to fulfil enough engagements and commitments to make it look like you had it together. That, and running. Running because you had said you would when things were better. But running, also, in an effort to escape where you'd left yourself.

Staring out of a train window one April weekend, you were jolted back into the world that had been passing you by. Pulled back into the present by a conversation you couldn't have avoided if you wanted to – such was the eardrum-testing decibel at which the two men seated opposite were holding court. And you wanted to avoid it. You wanted to look out unthinkingly at something that wasn't your flat, or your desk, or your commute. But no, with your cross-aisle companions projecting at that self-assured volume that only the middle-classes or RADA graduates are truly capable of, you had no choice but to eavesdrop.

"I can't wait for the World Cup, I'm so excited about it."

"I have to do the sweepstake at work, I run it."

"Who're you going for?"

"No… well… that's not how it works. It's a random draw."

"Do you rig it?"

"No. It's for fun, you know. I did the Euros one so…"

"…so you've made a profit so far?"

As they went on you had to quash the urge to interject, to correct the many mistruths, but also the urge to up and move. It would be too obvious; the carriage too sparse. So you sat, and you took it all in, and you remembered why it is you feel next to nothing for the sporting endeavours of the country you've lived in all your life, and instead throw everything you have into the country of your father. Humility over hubris.

"Can we at least get out of the group winning a game properly this time? Not like in 2010. Oh God, I mean remember that? When it was USA, Wales and Slovenia and we didn't even win a game! And then we went out to Germany, which was such bullshit. Four-one and it should've been two-all at half-time, and we'd have totally won that game. The Germans deflated, the boys loving it."

He clapped at that point. Actually clapped. Out loud. Five short, but firm claps. Like a branch manager of an office supplies company trying to gee up his sales team the morning after he's watched *The Wolf of Wall Street*.

"If we could have the attack we have now, but then Lampard and Gerrard, and the back four from 2002; Ashley Cole, Ferdinand, Gary Neville and who's the other one? The proper Tory, quality guy…"

"Sol Campbell?"

"Sol Campbell! That's it!"

If there were a camera to make a deadpan look to, you'd look to it. Instead you can only turn your gaze to the page of notes you had intended to make on this journey. The ones that were going to push you forwards, sort you out, draw you out of your hole. You've written just three words; 'buy recycling bin'. It's a start.

"Who's even in our group this time round? Belgium? I think we'll go through first. Easy."

If only you could channel such undaunted confidence, rather than continue to feel buried beneath a realism so heavy, most days you can barely make it above the surface to breathe.

The sweep

An email goes round. Electronic pings in headphones. A buzz of anticipation sweeps across the third floor. There are awkward stretches as hands go into pockets to fumble for loose change, or into bags in search of purses. People to whom you thought sport only existed as a topic to be avoided in Christmas games of Trivial Pursuit are getting excited. Names are written into a spreadsheet. Pound coins are handed over. Questions are asked.

"Who's in it?"

"How does it work?"

"Iran?!"

"Where's Italy?"

"Saudi Arabia; do they play football?"

"Ireland are usually in it aren't they?"

The spreadsheet slowly fills. First names typed in rectangles. An hour or so later, there's a plea for one last entrant.

"Only if I get Brazil."

"What is it?"

"Do I get to choose my team?"

A thirty-second pound coin is finally procured. There's the patter of sensible shoes, the squeak of desk chair wheels sent spinning backwards. Heads pop above screens. "Are they doing it now?" Emails are abandoned, cursors left flashing. Sixty-four feet hurry to the meeting table. The sweep is on and it's all in or nothing.

Audible reactions carry above the monitors to the far end of the office space; cheers, groans, oohs and aahs, a token shout of 'fix!' People return to their desks with small paper rectangles and a smile, a resigned look, or a question.

"Are Peru any good?"

"Iceland are decent now, right?"

"Who got England?"

Gradually a quietness is re-established; the sound of fingers moving over keyboards signalling a return to work, or perhaps just the hasty Googling of Nigerian odds and Serbian strike rates.

The wallchart

The day before the opening match, a tournament wallchart appears. One from the broadsheets. Beneath a shelf that carries faded industry magazines and a scanner that may or may not be broken, Blu-Tacked purposefully to the wall between reminders about correct font sizes and a press clipping with a favourable review. Throughout the morning colleagues, who in eight months haven't made so much as a passing reference to your Doncaster Rovers mug, get up from their desks and study the fixtures intently.

Tournament wallcharts always take you back to Euro 2000 and heading out to watch matches in the village pubs whose landlords were happy enough to turn a blind eye to the fact you were seventeen, just so long as you were handing over your money and behaving yourselves. Pints of Worthington Creamflow, bottles of Budweiser; England losing to Romania in The Station's back room, then going out to Portugal by the pool table in The Poacher.

You'd had wallcharts before that – on the back of bedroom doors; the side of a wardrobe. But Euro 2000 was your first collective effort. A *When Saturday Comes* one. Up proudly in the sixth form common room; taped to the breeze block wall behind your chair in the corner you and the other lads had just inherited from the departing upper sixth. Whilst the others came and went, from lessons and chip shop runs, you'd sit beneath it doing art coursework; tasked with the daily updates because yours was the neatest writing.

They tell you more than just the fixtures, wallcharts. The publications from which they originate give you an insight into the political and social background of their owner; their completion an indicator of commitment. Some are filled in attentively, others abandoned during the group stages, or the moment England go out. Some will come down in July, others will cling on into the autumn. At lunchtime, in the Argos on The Strand you spot another one; groups E-H of a tabloid giveaway poking out beyond the partition wall that shields the entrance to the back room. It surprised you a little. The people working there didn't look the sort to go in for *The Sun*, but there it was.

The group stages

Russia 5-0 Saudi Arabia

The World Cup begins at a set of traffic lights on Evelyn Street; upstairs on an idling 188 trying to work out why your Twitter feed is a succession of Robbie Williams gags. You are here because it's Thursday. And because Thursday is cognitive behavioural therapy day; forty-five minutes in a bunker of an NHS clinic – two-step intercom and barred windows – tucked among the towers and flat-roofed shops of a Deptford housing estate.

Your colleagues – unaware of where you disappear to on these weekly early finishes – will assume you've snuck off for the football; retreated from your desk to be on your sofa ready for the first match of sixty-four they expect you to be glued to. But the actuality is different. You don't own a sofa for one. And, instead of watching Clive Tyldesley attempt to somehow segue from children folk-dancing across the Luzhniki turf in sarafans to the selection headaches of Stanislav Cherchesov, you've been perspiring in a small consulting room decorated three shades of green, each more clinical than the last. Sitting in a standard issue comfortable chair at an unhelpfully low table, trying to understand why it is you've been thinking the way you've been thinking, and why you've spent so much of this year closing in on yourself.

You don't see the Russian anthem conclude to thunderous applause; you're 1,780 miles away from Moscow, and two miles from home, and you're on the wrong bus again. Come kick-off you're descending the escalator underground at Cutty Sark, squeezing past slow moving tourists to take the Docklands Light Railway back to Lewisham. When the train arrives, it is a mix of loosened ties and rolled-up sleeves – early office escapees and collected children. A man by the doors watches the match on his phone; the tinny noise of the crowd escaping his headphones and carrying towards you each time he turns his head to look out on the blur of high-rises and houses.

By the time you're putting your key in the front door of your flat, twenty-five minutes of the match have passed. However, your progress to the television is halted by a visitor. Lights all on. Clipboard in hand. He should've been done by now, but yet here he is, the man from the letting agents. Mid-term inspection. Have you really been here six months already? It still just feels like a place you retreat between days at work, a place to put your head down, somewhere you store your things. You're yet to think of it as a home.

"How's it been?" he asks. "Any issues?"

You consider laying it all on him, seeing how he takes it. He might be a good listener. But he probably just means the flat. And so you usher him down the stairs and out the door with a clumsy "Yeah fine... no real problems to be honest."

There are thirty-two minutes on the clock as you get your first true vista of World Cup action. It looks like a computer game, as big matches on the television so often do. All bright reds and greens and officially sanctioned hoardings; corporate uniformity over local identity. This game and this stadium could be anywhere in the world. You're too late for the opening goal, but in time to hear Glenn Hoddle clumsily intone that the VAR officials are watching on from the back of a van. It's an odd conclusion to reach, but certainly not the most questionable of his aired beliefs.

You find yourself shouting as Russia score their second, a Pavlovian cry of appreciation born out of Denis Cheryshev's neat sidestep and aesthetically pleasing lash into the roof of the net. The only noise you get back is the ding of bicycle bell out on the street below. The opening quarter of an hour of the second half is spent hoping for a Saudi Arabian riposte; something to keep the match in the balance, because you know how your attention tends to drift these days. Particularly here. Instead Russia make it three to wrap up the points, and so by the time they make it four, and then five, you're somewhere else entirely. In the room, but not the moment. The quality of the final two goals lost on you until tomorrow, when a text from a friend will encourage you to seek them out and watch them again. How could you have been dead to such a half-volley?

Egypt 0-1 Uruguay

On a nearby table three men are inhaling lager from plastic pint glasses as they discuss a mutual acquaintance who has clearly been taking liberties.

"Nah come of it mate, he's a cunt, everyone knows he's a cunt."

"At the end of the day he shouldn't be messaging my bird,

you know?"

"I'm not being funny Gal, you know, but he's basically a real cunt."

"I'm not having him making me look a mug like that though, you get me?"

"He aint worth it though, he's just a cunt."

"At the end of the day, I'm just gonna break his jaw or something."

Why, you wonder, must everything happen at dusk? The one they call Gal finishes his pint, squeezes the plastic in his hand and heads inside.

"Do you think anyone actually listens to him?" muses one of his mates in his absence.

"I do," replies the other. "When I'm on my own."

You didn't come here for the conversation. You're here because it's the only outdoor spot with WiFi strong enough to carry the match. Tray of food market dosa in hand, Martin Keown's punditry in ears, you initially plonked yourself in the considerably more serene environment of the roof garden. But what it held in ambience, it lacked in connectivity, bringing you only a mid-shout Fernando Muslera, pointing purposefully at the slow infinite turn of a loading wheel. So now you're on these tables overlooking the Thames; caught between the joyous yelps of children playing in the fountain, and the bloke-chat of would-be Danny Dyers kicking off their weekend.

Hunched over a tiny screen perhaps isn't the best way to enjoy the summer sunshine, but you've done enough aimless wandering this year. In mind and in body. Better to have a focus; a bit of structure. Your commitment to the first-half sadly doesn't yield a goal, despite Jonathan Pearce being convinced otherwise. As his ineptitude trends on Twitter you straighten your back and return to your desk, all the time wondering if anyone would notice if you didn't. You pass a quartet of Portugal shirts on Queen's Walk; a father and son playing in the fountain in dampened Spain jerseys. Everyone else is looking forwards.

Morocco 0-1 Iran

You're jogging east down the South Bank towards Blackfriars station. Side-stepping tourists who walk four abreast, hurdling errant children as they meander away from their parents, inhaling the sweet smell of caramelised nuts that lingers under Blackfriars Bridge. You're jogging because, just as you were about to leave your desk, Iran won a free-kick and you wanted to see how it panned out. Inevitably it came to nothing, save for this bout of unplanned exercise.

"Iran versus Morocco," a disappointed colleague had exclaimed late in the afternoon. "Who in their right mind would want to watch that?"

And you'd shrunk in your chair a little as you angled your laptop screen away from him and dragged your cursor to make the window in which you were watching the two teams enter the field that little bit smaller. Your jog ensures you make the train for the two-station-hop to Farringdon, checking on the score before the carriages burrow beneath the city. Still goalless.

At Finsbury Leisure Centre the interest in how things are

unfolding in St. Petersburg is more palpable than it had been in the office. Each familiar face who enters the subterranean changing room either provides the latest score or enquires about it. With phone signal unable to permeate the ground there is no room for empiricism; the last person to voice the score carries all authority.

After forty-five minutes of your own running and shooting and passing and dribbling and bobbles and mistakes and heckles and banter and "are we winning or is it still level?" you are back underground. Same seats, same lockers, only with heavier breath and damper clothes. Again reports are stilted – updated every few seconds like an oral Ceefax – and you listen to the picture unfold as you sit and empty rubber crumbs from your trainers.

"One nil."

"Own goal."

"...last minute apparently."

"No, Iran."

Later that night, unable to sleep again, your mind will wander to Iran's last World Cup victory; France '98, 2-1 over the USA. You don't need to look it up, and you remember the breakaway winning goal before you've flipped open the laptop and watched it all over again. First time round Mehdi Mahdavikia was bearing down on Kasey Keller in the living room of your mum's old semi-detached. A glare on the television screen from the conservatory windows; a South Yorkshire sunset cast across a rainy Lyon evening.

From here the floor falls away and you tumble down an internet rabbit hole to satisfy a need to know how they got to France. Why is it your focus only ever seems to thrive in the needless? As the city outside sleeps you prop yourself up on pillows, face illuminated against the darkened room by the screen, and familiarise yourself with the national football team of Iran circa 1997. Through bloodshot eyes you attempt to understand Arabic captions on their play-off draw in Sydney; you marvel at the ferocity of the goals they thundered in against China; you lie there wondering what it's like to be part of a partisan crowd of 100,000 or more – the football a distant dot beyond the running track, as you chant as one. All of you together.

Portugal 3-3 Spain

The Trader is busier than usual. The buzz of the Friday evening chatter is multilingual; Spanish, Portuguese and English bouncing back and forth across the small circles of people that fill out the floor space like liquid poured into a mould. There's laughter from tables where people in lanyards are embracing the weekend. Individuals sup up and stand, "another?" Arms are twisted, raised hands counted, before a careful edging between shoulders and over work bags, to get to the bar.

On the television above the fridges of the back bar is Cristiano Ronaldo – his face in close-up. He glances down at the optics and then stares straight ahead in concentration. The players are entering the field, but it's warm and you're sweating, so rather than find a gap beneath a screen you step out into the street, and join the others in leaning your bags against a lamppost and forming a misshapen circle. Above you, strung between pub wall and pub sign, the flags of Egypt, Saudi Arabia, Morocco and South Korea flap lightly in the breeze.

A loud noise from inside breaks conversation and eyes turn away from each other to peer inside the pub. Penalty. There are groans at a slow-motion replay. Half your group surge inside; you watch instead through the window. From the projector screen on the back wall Ronaldo surveys the pub's patrons, looks out towards the street, and then after a deep breath, starts his run up. The ball nestles in the corner of the net to a mixture of cheers and heckles. You all return to the lamppost, and back into a conversation about who's leaving and who isn't.

Another cheer, another chat abandoned to rush the doors and windows. Illuminated above the heads of those inside a man in dark red is holding his face and shouting at an official. You somehow know it is Pepe without being told. Now a man in silver is moving from left to right, and left to right, and shooting, and the ball is hitting the taut net and bouncing out again. One-all. Some of you now decide the game is too great a spectacle to be missed and find space inside, but it's still warm and still not yet dark, and so you stay by the lamppost. Talking. You don't get to talk often. Stilted conversations, but conversation nonetheless, held against the backdrop of oohs and aahs and gasps that roll out through the open pub doors.

Twenty minutes later another roar of noise. Discernible exclamations can be heard over the background of cheers and anger. "Oh no!" "What is that!?!" This time the television screens portray a pile of joyous bodies in officially sanctioned tabards, before the camera cuts to a man in green shaking his head and looking to the pub ceiling. A sense that you're missing something waves over the group and you pick up your bags, step through the doors and ease into the spaces vacated by half-time

15

smokers.

The pub is packed, you need to split up. Dotted about the room in twos and threes; the occasional tap on a shoulder as friends squeeze past, an offer of a drink, a grimace, a shake of the head, a "what a goal that was!" a "there can't be more in this can there?" Two-apiece. Three-two. The bodies in the pub continue to ebb and flow and rise and fall, and you'd forgotten how good it feels to be part of something where everyone is invested but ultimately nothing much matters.

Then, two minutes from time, a free-kick. Ronaldo's name carries through the pub expectantly, like a rumour of a lock-in.

"What do you reckon?" asks the friend in front of you.

"He'll score it," you say, "it's inevitable."

There's laughter and eye rolls as the number seven hitches his shorts up into hot-pants. A hush falls as he starts his run up, a second of absolute silence between the ball leaving his boot and stretching the net over the left shoulder of a frozen David De Gea. The pub is noise again. Strangers look at each other and shake their heads and take another drink. Your friend turns round to face you.

"Told you," you shrug, as if such certainty has ever come naturally.

France 2-1 Australia

If Greenwich is celebrating the World Cup then it's keeping

very quiet about it. The only sign that something, anything, might be different about this summer is a limp string of flags across the front of the sketchy Mexican restaurant on the corner; the one that doubles as a late night bar if you can find the right door to get upstairs and the bouncer doesn't mind your face – where they dish out bowls of chips until the early hours to satisfy a licensing loophole.

France and Australia have already been going at it for twenty minutes as you reach The Lost Hour. You contemplate walking on, but that familiar echoing noise of televised pub football – commentary bouncing between screens – draws you in. Flags of the World Cup nations are thumbtacked to the ceiling. You take a seat beneath Senegal and breathe in memories of past evenings spent here; football matches with your flatmate, birthday drinks surrounded by more people than you can remember. An embrace and a kiss for the surprise cake. Being told to break it up. You can picture being doubled over laughing in a window seat but can't recall what prompted it.

In the present it's not yet midday. You're drinking bad coffee. A trio of twenty-somethings are mulling over the best spot from which to watch the match, with a level of considered thought normally reserved for choosing a new dining table.

"No it's too glarey... is it not really glarey?"

"Nah, that one's too dark."

They walk and talk as they Goldilocks their way around the place in search of a screen that's just right. As they meander a first Australian chance sends a table's worth of hands to heads, silhouetted by the projected image of Hugo Lloris pumping his fists and preparing for a corner. Behind you a French couple look to each other in relief. Somewhere off to your left these two

17

worlds collide as a strong Australian accent wraps itself around the words "Gare du Nord". A Colombia shirt ambles down the stairs looking suitably lost.

Rather than struggle for a big screen sightline you watch the television the Goldilocks trilogy deemed too dark. Its contrast setting is off; the shadow of the near-side stand exaggerated so greatly that players and ball intermittently disappear into darkness and you can only guess their whereabouts by the reaction of those still in the light. As you wait for the ball to be lobbed back into your vision from what you assume to be a throw-in, an old man takes a seat beneath the monitor. He rests his cap on the chair next to him, places his pint carefully on a beer mat, and shakes open his newspaper. Peering thoughtfully at each article through his thick black-framed glasses, he licks his left thumb before every turn of the page.

As he reads, the rest of the room rises in volume. The tournament's first need for VAR has brought discussion and anticipation to the pub and drawn passers-by to an open window; faces squinting through the frame in an unwitting mimic of the referee peering at a touchline monitor. The official turns back to the pitch and points deliberately toward the penalty spot, his professionalism shining through as he remains completely unswayed by the protests of a distant Greenwich pub.

The second half rolls away from there. A woman stands up in front of the big screen and is shouted down playfully by the whole bar. The cast of people watching at the window alternates like visitors passing through an aquarium. You're surprised to hear the French shout "Yes!" instead of "Oui!" An Aussie voice keeps shouting "Come on Ryan!" and throughout it all, even through the huge cheer and stamping of feet that greets the

Australian equaliser, the old man sits unmoved, carefully and deliberately picking his way through his newspaper, the beer in his glass having barely dipped below the pint mark.

Argentina 1-1 Iceland

You're keen to take in every game, but have little want to do so in the confines of your flat. And so you push on by train, two stops to London Bridge. Here on winter Saturday mornings you play guess the club with the scarves, shirts, and hats that blur through the station concourse. Today there is only a solitary Argentina to be seen, distinctive sky-blue and white stripes atop a denim skirt, standing at a bureau de change, foot tapping impatiently. On you go, down to Elephant & Castle, to that small tucked away football bar you discovered with the friend you inherited from the relationship.

Where once there were flats, a huge expanse of affordable, liveable flats, now there is a building site, shiny hoardings, and this collection of brightly painted shipping containers converted into food outlets, coffee shops and bars. A spirit of entrepreneurship for those with little to lose. You lament the loss of the housing, but not enough to boycott the bar. You're a hypocrite; your only defence that in London it's hard not to be.

The Six Yard Box is decorated with football stickers and stray magazine pages. Tiny faces of past World Cup tournaments stare down at you from the ceiling. Over your shoulder a Marseille-era Eric Cantona is in mid-flight; shiny white and sky blue nylon glistening against a floodlit night.

Outside in the courtyard a crowd fresh off an architectural drawing for a new creative hub gathers around a flat-screen television wheeled from a store cupboard. Rather than hang awkwardly at its periphery you opt instead for a spot inside and the guarantee of a seat and a table out the way.

Aside from the barman only three other people have chosen the dark over the light. Two Norwegians and a Korean. All are supporting Iceland, as too – going by the yells of encouragement that carry through the open door with every Icelandic foray into the opposition half – are the majority of those outside.

"I support all the Norwegian countries," says one of the big lads beneath the screen, repatriating Scandinavia during a brief pause between gulps of Pilsner.

At half-time the Korean and louder of the Norwegian pair chat. You listen in. They are Tottenham and Arsenal respectively; neither a fan of football in their home country – the previous warmth of briefly adopted Icelandic nationhood that connected them cools. You're tempted to join in, break from your isolation, stop being the quiet bloke in the corner, but you can't. You can't find the words to follow an initial interjection. You find it too hard. It gets you anxious. When and how did you forget how to chat?

During the second-half, their group swells in number and nations; a Swede and a Spaniard join them, followed by a pair of Danes with two French bulldogs. Though their owners may be caught up in a multi-national natter, the dogs do not go short of attention. Each and every person walking to the bar takes a moment to stoop and stroke or fuss the pair, before looking up to ask a question.

"Are these yours?"

"What are their names?"

"How old are they?"

"Are they related?"

In half an hour the only person not to deviate dogwards from their path to the bar is you.

Penalty. The chatter falls silent. The latest dog-petter stands up. A close up of Lionel Messi as he faces the goalkeeper. He has to score, he's bound to score. "Messi don't miss these, fam!" shouts someone beyond the door. But, as a hearty roar carries from outside, echoing across the building sites and bouncing off the windows of empty luxury apartments, he does. His penalty saved. The match drawn. This very recently established district of Little Reykjavik satisfied.

Peru 0-1 Denmark

You pass the Colombian cafes wedged under the railway arches of Elephant & Castle, each of them filling with interest in the fortunes of their cross-border cousins. Into the lift and a slow descent among strangers, down into the cool dank of the Underground. On the train to London Bridge a row of Peruvian shirts slide past the windows waiting to board at Borough. You contemplate following, staying on the train and going where they're going, pursuing an atmosphere, or at least an anecdote.

But you're tired. You've hardly slept. Again. And so one stop later the roles are reversed, you stand on the platform as the distinctive red sashes blur past you from behind the glass of a Tube carriage, off to find a slice of Lima on the Northern Line.

In Lewisham, four lads are ambling across the parkland at the end of Elmira Street; carrier bags in hands, bucket hats on heads. They look worse for wear.

"Nah, we should make the most of it," you hear one say, "it's the only day where there's four games on. You get me?"

"We've already missed two of them, what does it matter?" asks his friend, but they carry on regardless. Determined, in a lazy way, to achieve at least half of their day's aims.

You hang your washing on an airer in the living room as the players sing their anthems, and marvel at the sheer volume of Peruvian support. A town's worth of people who have upped and travelled across oceans and continents to be part of something. A first chance in a generation, gleefully grabbed. Here in South London you struggle to show anywhere near the same level of resolve. It's a breathless end-to-end game, but the effects of little sleep and last night's online Iranian history delve are kicking in. You find yourself unable to concentrate, again. Staring beyond the screen to somewhere in the past; pulled out of it briefly by Christian Cueva's hapless penalty and Yussuf Poulsen's breakaway goal, but ultimately dwelling instead of digesting.

Croatia 2-0 Nigeria

It's a sunny evening in appearance, but not temperature. Families play in Ladywell Fields in a golden evening light, but you're wearing a thick shirt and didn't get more than thirty yards from home before unrolling the sleeves. Behind the wire-covered windows on each of the two barbershops at the top of Doggett Road the game beams out from a flatscreen on the wall. At the first, a man stands and watches from the door; in the second a big guy in a green shirt laughs heartily, to the amusement of the barber and his fellow customers, whilst Nigerian fans in elaborate costume bounce about on the screen behind him.

In Catford Bridge Tavern you meet a couple of friends; a couple you helped facilitate. It's good to see them both, but it's hard not to feel like a hanger on, an accompaniment, an appendage. For a Saturday night, the pub is quiet; the match dominates the wall to your right, but few are watching it; the three of you, a couple of guys at the bar, half a date, a middle-aged man lounging in a 1970s recliner, whisky perched on the arm.

Occasionally people waiting at the bus stop outside peer in to check the score or kill the wait. Nigeria disappoint. You'd expected more, but they're going at it like a friendly and things are flat as a result, both in Kaliningrad and here in Catford. Conversation is relaxed, but sparse. You've not hung out in months but have little to catch up on. Time has passed, but you've stood still, and so your chatter has all the fluidity and purpose of Nigeria's attack; offering little to nothing until it's too late.

As you leave the pub the sky is in the final throes of daytime; a crimson tinge hinting at an earlier sunset. In the new apartments where Catford Dog Track used to be, cats slink silently between neatly ordered foliage; people sit and talk on bamboo fringed balconies and patios in the fading light, illuminated by fairy lights or candles. Beyond the late evening dog-walkers on Ladywell Fields and along Malyons Road, a single England flag flutters on the rooftop of a gardener's van. A fake Christmas tree, tinsel and all, lays on its side in the road; a family talk on their front step.

The shutters are down in Ladywell, save for the bright lights of the chicken shop – where two men in red hats lean on the counter waiting for business – and the salon two doors down where hairdressers chat with their final customers. Delivery drivers and cyclists sit on the bench outside the pizza restaurant, smoking away the remainder of their shift, an empty bus rounds the corner and crests the railway bridge. On Algernon Road an alarm bleeps once as a man turns away from his car with a carrier bag wedged beneath each arm, he steps into his hallway and elbows his front door closed behind him. The street lamps flicker on.

Costa Rica 0-1 Serbia

It's a grey and breezy summer Sunday, but Hackney is still Hackney. Coffee shops do ample trade; outdoor tables packed with brightly coloured anoraks and exposed ankles, and tiny dogs looking expectantly at croissants and cronuts. A headless mannequin in a charity shop window wears an old Ugandan football shirt. Outside the Christ Power International Ministry on Belsham Street stands a congregation in their Sunday best; elaborate yet impeccable headscarves and dresses at odds, in their riots of primary colours, with the run-down former warehouse behind them.

Inevitably for contemporary East London, World Cup themed pop-ups have filled otherwise empty shops and units; one sells fashion inspired by football, the other sells football that has become fashion. You head into the latter via a confused interaction with the man offering low-level security at the door – him asking if you have a ticket, before telling you that you don't need one. Painted white walls, concrete floor, a big screen and benches, racks of old football shirts, draft pints in plastic cups. Your friend who's always late is late. But you knew this before reaching to your pocket for his apologetic message. It's why you didn't run for that bus in Dalston.

You've both had difficulties with your mental health this past year. His have been more public than yours. He will talk openly about his on social media with a bluntness that can sometimes make you a little uncomfortable. Not least because often you first learn about it from other people asking you if he's all right. You don't begrudge him, we all have to find a way to cope and you respect that this is his. But it's a difficult space to occupy, attempting to be there for someone, and assure others that you are supporting that person, because they view you as being in some way strong when the actuality is you yourself are desperately trying to cling to being something, anything approaching OK.

It's an unwritten understanding that when you meet up and watch football, it's an escape. A chance to get away from the

25

negativity that hangs over your respective brows and lose yourself in something else. Which is fine. You do need that, and so you go along with it. But he has a loving wife; close support and human contact. And often, beyond the 'please' and 'thank you' of a financial transaction, you haven't had a conversation in a week, possibly longer. And so your feelings and your mood, and your concern and your fears remain unspoken of. Trapped until professional intervention.

You're supporting Costa Rica, that's the premise for this. Him not long back from honeymoon there; you enamoured with any country that sees no need for an army and values literacy over conflict. But the game is uneventful and your chat nudges events on the screen into the background. The fortunes of these two football nations only ever becomes a main draw during his cigarette breaks. The wedding, the honeymoon, the football, the shirt-based nostalgia. Costa Rica will have other games, who knows when you'll next get chance for idle conversation.

Germany 0-1 Mexico

You each take a time out before the second game of the day. Him for a cigarette, and to buy more cigarettes. You for an underwhelming sandwich from a hectic supermarket, packed with families trying to corral bored children through a big shop. You eat by the roadside, leant against a wall, watching shoppers run for buses, and looking up at the council flats opposite, wondering who lives in them and what things they can see from the uppermost windows.

Back in the pop-up shirt store, you've secured the same table and sit in the same order, drinking the same drinks, talking about the same things. Only this time there's keener interest in the match from you and the wider bar, and in particular from a German family at the next table. The four of them are decked out in retro football shirts of your childhood; the national team bookended by Bayern Munich and Borussia Dortmund respectively. And so now, with the game more engaging, your chat fills the gaps in action, rather than the action filling the gaps in your chat.

Mexico are good. Really good. The vintage-shirted Germans are able to laugh off the first unsuccessful Mexican raid on their nation's goal with theatrical mimes of relief, but as the counter-attacks keep coming you watch their confidence dissipate into concern. When Hirving Lozano scores after thirty-five minutes it sparks joy so unconfined in Mexico City that seismographs register the reaction to the goal as an earthquake. Here in Hackney the celebrations are muted in comparison, the ground doesn't shake, but at least one beer is spilt and the cheers cause would-be shoppers to abandon the racks of shirts and turn to the screen for the replays. "We're all Mexico!" shouts your friend, caught up in the moment, earning a withering look from the adjacent table.

You *are* all Mexico though; it's a hook to hang your involvement on. For you it's an eternal empathy with the underdog. For others it's an irrational dislike of Germany; a constructed rivalry that has to be justified or – in the case of the guy in sunglasses leaning against the wall behind you telling his friend "I don't hate Germany, I quite admire them" – played down. Germany press. The action increasingly takes place on the left-hand side of the projection. "Fuck off, fuck off, fuck off, fuck off!" shouts your friend each time Germany threaten the

27

Mexican goal. You don't just want Mexico to hold out, you need them to. You need some collective joy.

There are cheers as Manuel Neuer goes forward; the entire space rubbernecking on the anguish being felt by the room's sole Germanic table. They seem good people. No-one wishes ill on them. But everyone likes a story; the bits where football loses its predictability. The clock ticks away. The ball glances a post. Joachim Low's hands go to his head. The referee's whistle goes to his mouth. The bar cheers. There's a high-five. And then you all, one by one, up and leave and go about your day.

Brazil 1-1 Switzerland

On the pavement outside New Cross Gate station a man in a bowler hat plays the theme from *The Pink Panther* on the saxophone. It raises a smile, and you fumble in your pocket for loose change for his cup. Not the pound coins, but everything smaller. You get off the bus at the wrong stop again; still unable to get used to which number stops where. The weather has dropped and cooled, the sky is overcast and the wind is whipping at your t-shirt sleeves as you retrace the last few hundred yards of the bus route, past a man arguing demonstratively into his phone, treating the bus shelter as a provincial theatre for his one-man recital of the righteous big man.

Ten minutes are gone by the time you turn on the television. Brazil are on the front foot. Neymar is soon on the floor. The ball is soon in the net. It's a one-sided half without chances, and your attention soon wanders again. From your kitchen you can hear people in a back garden two doors down steadfastly having a barbecue. The sound of chatter and feet on gravel; the smell of smoke and sausages. You're back in the room when Switzerland equalise. And you listen as on screen analysis slides into a debate on VAR; within a few minutes a moment that briefly brought a nation together has had every ounce of fun analysed out of it until you realise you're no longer watching and it's getting dark outside and another weekend has gone.

Sweden 1-0 South Korea

"Who's winning?" asks the woman that sits directly behind you.

"It's nil-nil," replies a colleague.

"Yeah, but who's winning?"

"No-one, it's nil-nil, neither side have scored."

You're working off two screens, the larger monitor purely a decoy to divert attention away from the smaller one upon which you're watching the match. Spreadsheets and word documents pulled to the edges of your window on Russia as camouflage, just in case someone more senior than you comes over. You don't get much done, but then little you do here seems to carry any urgency anyway. You watch the penalty that settles the game and do little to disguise your watching of the rest of the half.

"So, did we win?" asks the Swedish person who sits over your left shoulder, returning to her desk. A national interest in a sport she doesn't care for, but it's enough to separate one Monday afternoon from all the others.

Belgium 3-0 Panama

Your Outlook calendar has just two entries, wedged together in a sea of digital grey. Your only two meetings deftly crammed back to back between 3pm and 4pm, so you can be back at your desk to listen to the day's second game. Time manipulated to try and eke some enjoyment from a working day. However, come 4pm the mischievous thrill and excitement of following the football from your office chair is soon offset as Mark Lawrenson's futility is ferried directly into your ears. It's like bunking off school, just to go to an alternative school.

Your belief that your office World Cup watching is anything approaching clandestine is shown to be wishful thinking as, over the course of an hour, three different colleagues ask you the score. You can plan, but you can't hide.

"Three-nil now," you reply to the third ask, prompting a multi-desk discussion as to who has Belgium in the sweepstake, and a colleague to wander over to the wallchart for confirmation. No-one has strong feelings for or against Belgian success, but at the same time no-one wants someone they don't particularly like to be its beneficiary.

Tunisia 1-2 England

You emerge from the office into a humid summer evening, one bereft of sunshine, but high on anticipation. Bass notes carry on the breeze from the middle of the River Thames where a Budweiser-backed bar boat is bringing beery blokes down the water. From the throng of England shirts on the deck, pint glasses and plastic flags are raised to the air for a chorus of *'Seven Nation Army'* before the vessel disappears under Hungerford Bridge.

The walk along the South Bank is thinner of folk than normal. A handful of England shirted men walk briskly towards lager and large screens, but otherwise it's just the international chatter of tourists, hands-free phone calls of evening commuters, and the melancholy guitar of buskers outside Tate Modern. Your destination was The Scoop, where you'd anticipated an outdoor screen showing the game. Instead it hosts a dance class; teenage girls and Indian beats where you expected to find anthems and encouraging applause.

By the time you pass The Draft House on Tower Bridge Road the match is underway; the pub packed to the door with people fresh from nearby offices. Shoulder-blades against the windows, necks craning to distant screens. You carry on down the street; at your back a crescendo of anticipation followed by a groan tells you England have gone close to opening the scoring as you turn down Boss Street.

You get your first glimpse of the action through the doors of The Kings Arms; the match playing out above a couple of hundred heads. A friend is inside – you can see her through the window – but it's not worth the discomfort. You stay put on the pavement, watching through an open fire door, even though the television you can see is angled so unfavourably it's four minutes before you realise it's actually Tunisia who are in white. England take the lead. Through the glass a man in a Bobby Moore number six shirt rises from his seat with his arms aloft before Harry Kane has even struck. Cheers, and applause, raised glasses. A couple of guys wheeling suitcases down the street take a breather next to you to watch the replay; a child swings on the bicycle racks.

In the reception of Downside Fisher Youth Club, a group of kids and a couple of staff watch the match on a small television placed high on a corner shelf. They're joined by adults arriving for the Monday night dodgeball league, of which you are one. Different people of different ages united by a common silence of anticipation as the referee blows his whistle and points to the penalty spot.

"Oh my days, how is that even a penalty?" asks a young kid in a Millwall shirt, whilst you try and explain VAR to your non-football following friend. The officials don't share the kid's doubt and the ball is swept home to a collective groan and one of the other children joking, "I'm an immigrant though. I'm an immigrant though, so it doesn't matter if England lose. I'm not properly English."

It's still 1-1 by the time you finish throwing balls about; the kids still sit beneath the television, the Kings Arms is still full to the doors. You decide not to stay, and walk on down Tooley Street, catching up on the lives of your friends and teammates, and using the reactionary noises from the pubs you pass to determine the score. Through the windows of The Shipwrights Arms a row of white-collar shirts, traces of sweat in the lower back; their owners peering through the strings of celebratory flags that hang above the bar to get a view of the screen. Another audible near miss carries from the pub as you stand by the entrance to London Bridge station.

"Do you not want to catch the last ten minutes?" you ask a friend.

"No, I'm over them," he says, "I can't be doing with another summer of them letting me down."

You're on a train, arriving at St. John's station, as the winning goal goes in. No hint at a repeat of the earthquake that shook Mexico yesterday; here your surroundings are unmoved. On a platform bench two drunken older men sit talking, here in the carriage the only noise is a woman on the phone, lying about being "just outside Eltham now Barb, be fifteen minutes, yeah." The game is done as you alight at Lewisham; the noise of a couple of excited female voices shouting "Two one!" and "Eng-ger-land!" carries through the booking hall from platform three, but otherwise, as sensible shoes mind the gap and Oyster cards tap out, it's the end of any other Monday commute, just with fewer people.

Colombia 1-2 Japan

'Colombia v Japan has got off to some start,' you read on a tweet as you sit on the upper deck of the 171. You quickly tap and scroll to find a live stream, and as the bus sits in traffic outside The Old Vic you shield your phone screen from the sun to watch Shinji Kagawa roll the penalty into the net before running towards a corner flag kissing the crest on his shirt, disappearing behind a blur of bodies leaping about on the touchline as he goes.

Where the afternoon light refracts off the tiled walls of Elephant & Castle station's Bakerloo entrance, a couple of Colombia shirts walk purposefully down the pavement; bright yellow spots on a monochrome afternoon in the capital. These, it transpires, are merely the first snowflakes of a heavy fall. Across the street, in Elephant & Castle Shopping Centre, the yellow of Colombia is everywhere; shirts are worn by shoppers, restaurateurs and hairdressers, they hang from racks in convenience stores and are pinned to the wall in cafes.

Looking down from the walkway that connects the Centre to the station, a blur of yellow-clad bodies can be seen through the perspex roof of Leños & Carbon. Beyond the beeps of Oyster Card readers and automated apologies for late running services, the businesses beneath the railway arches are showing the game; all of them. Whether bar, restaurant, cafe, grocers or sex-shop, each has a Colombian flag in the window, and a scrum of yellow shirts at its door, peering inside to watch a distant television set. With only the sex shop offering anything close to a navigable entrance, you cross the street and squeeze into the Lost River Brewery. It isn't Colombian. Not ordinarily. Today however it is as yellow and fervent as its surroundings.

Colombians of all ages cram the space; all of them wearing national team shirts. You feel like the one person to have turned up to a Halloween Party not in costume.

"Where is your shirt?" a woman asks you at the bar.

"I know, I should have one."

"Ah you are English."

"No, Welsh."

"And today?"

"Oh, today I am Colombian."

"Good answer," she replies and merges back into the crowd.

And what a crowd. Under the bigger of the two screens sit a couple in elaborate yellow, red and blue hats; a variety of horns and traditional pastries laid out on the table in front of them. A man is using a motorcycle helmet as a drum, there are people decked in flags so decoratively embroidered they look like they've been lifted from an embassy boardroom. A bottle of a traditional spirit is passed from table to table with diminishing secrecy. Young couples are face-timing relatives, older men take photos on huge tablets.

The animation around you distracts from a poor Colombian performance, but just before half-time they get a free-kick, one they really need to score. They do so. The ball squeezing over the line, and the celebration rises as a crescendo as more and more people realise that yes, it is indeed a goal. Horns are blown, air horns blasted, hats go in the air, flags are waved with vigour; shirts are clasped by fingers taught with joy.

At half-time, people escape their tense humid rooms and flood outside in search of air. The brewery crank up their Latin American playlist and turn their speakers to face out into the square. Yellow shirts and beats abound, a ball is kicked about; everyone is smiles. Up above, people on platform four of Elephant & Castle station pop their heads over the fence to try and make sense of the commotion below. Here, on the apron of gentrification, for fifteen minutes at least, people are reclaiming their space in the area they've been forcibly priced out of. Right now this is Colombia. It is rough, and ready, and a genuinely joyous thing to be part of.

It's almost a shame to spoil it all with another half of football, but a horn blown from inside the Brewery signals the start of the second forty-five minutes, and people stream back into the premises from which they'd previously spilled. The primary horn-blower is a middle-aged woman sat beneath the screen; stoic faced but persistent, she blows it over and over again until her sons get embarrassed and then she bursts out laughing. A short old man moves around the bar complaining to everyone and anyone that he cannot see the screen, all whilst never really doing anything to try and rectify the issue.

The cheer that greets the introduction of James Rodriguez' as a substitute is almost as loud as that which met the goal. Flags waved, horns horned, a chant of "Olé, Olé, Olé". But Colombia have long been penned in their half, and the goal Japan have been chasing – to a local soundtrack of wary screams and shouted defensive advice – eventually arrives to stub out the atmosphere. The horns are put away. At full-time people file out into the daylight once again, but the congregation this time is more that of a wake than a party; firm handshakes and consolatory shrugs. The old couple who'd optimistically unfolded a souvenir table on the square get glances but little trade.

Poland 1-2 Senegal

Your plan to watch each of today's games with invested spectators threatens to fall down in Holborn where Bar Polski is bereft of both people – Polish or otherwise – and of live football. You pause on a bench in Lincoln's Inn Fields to consider your next move over a supermarket sandwich. A smattering of people lie on the grass, a man and woman move past walking and talking business, a homeless man ushers his dog into the trees.

You take a punt on heading west and descend into the sultry warmth of the Central Line, swaying four stops by the doors before emerging at Marble Arch. A couple of left turns, a couple of rights and into The Carpenter's Arms, an old school boozer that refuses to follow the pace of gentrification around it; shunning the Scandi Chic refits of nearby cafes and shops of indeterminable goods, for a mismatch of upholstered stools, abrasive service and heavy beer-soaked tables.

You've struck lucky. Beneath the big-screen half a dozen big Polish men perch on high stools and lean against the windowsill. Polski scarves are draped over chairs, necks and laps. They're into the game, but rarely get animated by it. You're not supposed to drink before your sessions, but reason you can allow yourself one pint at this hour, and place it carefully on a wobbly wooden table, facing a small corner television. Through the window you watch people from nearby businesses take their breaks in the adjacent Mews, leaning against the wall opposite the pub and alternating between cigarette drags and mobile apps.

Senegal take the lead in slow motion; Thiago Cionek's deflection carrying the ball into the bottom corner to near silence in the pub. The only reaction being three of the Polish men turning abruptly on their heels to seek solace in smoke. As you watch the replays, their clouds of consolation billow up past the hanging baskets beyond the glass.

At half-time the pub's clientele doubles, people clocking out of offices at 5pm on the dot and straight to the bar. One of the younger Polish lads translates a lager order for an older contemporary. Two female students make you feel old as they root around in their bags for ID. Polish fortunes fail to improve and the match ebbs away uneventfully save for an all too late consolation.

Full-time brings a yell of "Fuck!" from beneath the screen, and another collective traipse outside. As you leave you pass two of the Polish fans on the steps of the building across the Mews, silently, sullenly, glaring at the floor between inhalations.

Italy 1990

Seven-years-old and playing round Scott's house; his dad's laughter carrying from the living room where he's watching Rene Higuita's sweeper-keeper routine backfire for Colombia against "the Macaroons." The bright yellows and greens. Roger Milla's celebration that ensured every goal in the playground from then until the summer holidays was followed by a run away to a nearby tree, a wiggle of the hips and a skinny white arm in the air.

Not quite hooked on football enough to grasp what was happening; Rudi Voller and Frank Rijkaard's spat passed you by, you didn't see David Platt's hooked volley, nor Gary Lineker's blurred close-up asking for Bobby Robson to have a word with him. But you had a toy car, a white Fiat with the Ciao figure on the bonnet and 'Italia '90' on the roof. The red white and green mini-football too - yours successfully plucked from one of those grabbing machines outside an arcade on Scarborough's South Bay. You wonder what became of it. It's probably still on your primary school roof, faded and worn, goal-kicked into eternal stasis.

Russia 3-1 Egypt

On Edgware Road there is little doubting the main draw of this World Cup summer. Behind the men who sit at the street-side shisha tables huge action shots of Mo Salah adorn the wall outside of Shishawi restaurant. Horns sound, not because of the traffic, but because taxi drivers have seen friends or national shirts on the pavement. Waves, fist clenches; two young guys trail an Egyptian flag behind them as they turn down George Street; Salah's face looks out from another cafe window.

You traverse the length of the street and back again, unable to find the confidence to cross a threshold and join the expectant crowds, even though it's why you're here. Kick-off approaches as you make your return journey along the pavement; in a jewellers the players enter the field; in a mobile phone shop they line up for the anthems; in a busy cafe the match gets underway over the heads of people waiting to be seated. You walk on to Paddington Basin and settle onto a stool in a much less partisan chain pub at the end of the water, nurturing a lemonade throughout the first half whilst listening to a big bearded American loudly talking about how "I guess I just don't want to reduce my salary."

By the time Russia take the lead you're in a fourth floor room on the corner of Little Venice. You're looking out a window, across the algae covered water of the canal's convergence, at clouds turned orange by the sun as it drops behind the houses and church spires of Maida Vale and the high-rises of Latimer Grove. You're not watching the football. You're crying. Not at the spectacle of a city sunset, but because this is counselling. Therapy by another name. An attempt to get on top of your depression that, whilst helping, has been getting harder and harder each week.

You're crying because the therapist has asked you to list the qualities of the woman you loved and because with each one you realise you are listing another facet that's lost from your life, and you're grieving not only the loss of a person, but of compassion and companionship and support and connectivity and – as it feels at this moment – any chance of having those aspects in your life again. You try and fight the tears because you know you can't talk when you're crying.

"You don't have to talk," says your therapist, "you can just sit," and you turn to the window again to see a dozen balloons released from behind a building just off the west towpath of the canal. As their silhouettes drift up silently across the flaming sky you wipe the water from your cheeks and try to go again.

Egypt are out by the time you are. There will be no celebrations on the Edgware Road to pull you out of your sullen regret; instead it's just a delayed Tube, a beatboxing Spaniard on the platform, and an attempt to at least make it home before you collapse in on yourself again.

Portugal 1-0 Morocco

Only the promise of another carefully engineered half day has managed to pull you out of bed and into work. You spend as much of your four hour shift as possible in the safety of your headphones; avoiding conversation, avoiding the need to be anything to anyone. Just trying to keep typing quicker than your

41

brain can fall away into thoughts that aren't for here.

You re-emerge from the audio comfort blanket of funk and soul to one of your colleagues asking if anyone has ever scored back-to-back hat-tricks at a World Cup; a question which indirectly informs you Ronaldo has already opened the scoring. You're tied to your desk for thirty more minutes; but in between typed sentences you pause to rattle off scoring feats and statistics from past World Cups that you really shouldn't know off pat. Just Fontaine scored thirteen at the 1958 tournament; Oleg Salenko scored five against Cameroon in 1994; Hakan Sukur scored the quickest goal, against South Korea in 2002. Safety in numbers.

Outside the sun is shining on those emerging from offices to take a late lunch – the heat enhanced by the fresh tarmac they're laying on Belvedere Road. Supermarkets do a roaring sandwich trade, the friendly *Big Issue* seller on Stamford Street bids you a good afternoon and you respond in kind, feeling guilty that you bought your copy from the grumpier one up on Hungerford Bridge.

On Southwark Street you spot a familiar face from your past. It takes you a moment to pinpoint where, but slowly it comes to you; university, a woman you once dated, very tall, very blond, very attractive. You remember her getting terribly drunk on a date. Propping her up as you swayed down the pavement on Portland Street; clumsily trying to ensure she at least got in her front door before you set off back across the city. You contemplate breaking into a jog to catch up and say hello, but your memory keeps whirring on and you remember the reason it never went beyond a few dates; her surprisingly latent racism. You don't jog. You let her disappear into the revolving door of a glass office block and you press on.

42

In Flat Iron Square the air is a cocktail of smokes – cigarette from those watching the game, grill and barbecue from the vans and gazebos that offer food from the fringes. The sun beats down and trains rumble over the arches. People in office-wear mix with groups draped in Portuguese flags and scarves. A toddler plays with toys in the shade beneath a table; the occasional breeze wafts away the burning sensation from your arms as you sit in the bright sunshine.

On the vast screen at the end of the square Cristiano Ronaldo is playing the role of pantomime villain; known by everyone, the reactions to his appearance are intrinsic and dependent on nationality. The Portuguese cheer his expressions and his gestures, the rest of the world wince and groan. Once again he is starring in the soap opera Ronaldo, directed by Ronaldo, screening daily in the mind of Ronaldo; everyone else – the opposition, his teammates, the officials, you, the people around you – merely his audience. He signals a request for VAR making a screen around his face; a metaphor for his existence. Watch me again, in close up, in slow motion, and from every angle.

Morocco have sympathisers in the square, but only one fan. A man, alone, seated prominently, just to the left of the action. He wears a vintage Morocco tracksuit and strokes his stubbled face pensively throughout; omnipresent in the bottom corner of your view as if he's offering sign language of the action. Much to his frustration Morocco remain close but not close enough, knocking frequently on the door, but never finding a way in, like a mid morning cold-caller.

Uruguay 1-0 Saudi Arabia

On Union Street, Southwark, a well-to-do middle-class couple in a cosy coffee shop talk loudly to each other, and their tiny dog, with the outward confidence wealth seems to nurture. Even with headphones on and music turned up, you cannot help but pick up snippets of their conversation.

"...he expects me to look after the annex I suppose..."

"...no, it cost me three grand in the end..."

"...is no-one paying you attention sausage?"

"...would you believe it? He adores that man with the tattoos on his face, but he won't go near the nice lady in the card shop."

You sigh, finish your drink quicker than intended, and decide to head back south east to watch the game. On the corner of St. Thomas Street you pass a girl in her late teens looking at her phone screen and telling her friends "we've got half an hour 'til the match kicks off." You sidestep a charity fundraiser's joviality and get a train out to New Cross. It's warm, and you can feel sweat drops forming on your forehead as the train rattles past The Den.

You remember The Royal Albert has a television now and cross the street to try the door. It's locked. It's five minutes past the opening time, but when the draw of a pub is its laid back approach, you can hardly take offence at it taking the same ethos to opening. You could have asked the woman unchaining the outdoor tables, she probably would have opened the doors, but you hate to feel like you're imposing, even when you're not, and so you turn on your heels and head to the DLR.

Luis Suarez' goal midway through the first half catches you out – the rise in volume of the commentary drawing you back down the hallway to stand idly by the door with a tea-towel in your hands as you watch the replay. Mohammed Al-Owais flapping at a corner he was never going to reach; Suarez merely angling his foot to divert the ball goalwards and then running, grinning towards a camera by the corner flag. You go back to the kitchen.

Iran 0-1 Spain

You feel like heading out to watch this one, but where would you go? There's no-one nearby who shares an interest, and the pub at the end of the road has prioritised the weekly quiz night over group games. Home alone again you throw yourself into the plight of the underdog to try and feel a connection. This time at least, it seems to pay off, and so when Karim Ansarifard flashes a volley into the side netting you find yourself returning his reaction of hands-on-head anguish. An involuntary shout of "oooh" carrying from your mouth out the open window and into the evening street below.

When Spain ruin the moment a minute later, scoring with a ricochet off Diego Costa's knee, you fear that hope and interest will soon fade, but Iran mercifully hook you back in. A free-kick. A flick-on. A scramble. A scuff goalwards. And suddenly Iranian players are running in every direction. Substitutes are on the field, a hat is thrown in the air in front of the camera. But just as you're laughing along, the camera cuts to a close-up of an official with his arm in the air. Offside. A video consultation. Joy evaporated by technological efficiency.

Iran don't give up, and you persevere with them to the last. It's the most you've connected with a game in your own home so far. Enthused by Iranian endeavour, you pull on your trainers and go for a late evening run. Your first in weeks, maybe a month; reconnection with what had been your crutch in navigating the darkness of the winter months.

Through the streets and into the park. You run beneath a perfect half moon and purple chemtrails behind twinkling planes. You run past weed smokers on playground equipment, and one final family packing up blankets and balls. The beat of indie music in your ears to drown out your heavy breaths and clicking ankle joints, singing along silently, "Did you notice when you began to disappear? Was it slowly at first?"

Denmark 1-1 Australia

"VAR strikes again," says a colleague as you're heading out the door, but you've already logged off. You're leaving early on the premise of another session of cognitive behavioural therapy, but the reality is the previous week's was your last. Not through choice. You felt it helpful, that it was working for you, but only four weeks in, your therapist is leaving the UK. The uncertainty of life beyond next year prompting a hasty move back to her home country. And so whilst you wait to be reassigned to another therapist, to begin all over again, you choose not to say anything of this change to your employers, and for a few more weeks at least embrace the excuse for a summer afternoon away from your desk.

The Mulberry Bush in Southwark is close, but quiet. The match plays out silently on a single screen as television executives from across the road finish long lunches with little urgency. The barman has enough time between customers to make idle conversation about the continuing good weather; you spend the stumbled chat trying to pinpoint his accent but concede defeat, before taking a seat on a sofa beneath the screen.

You're too late for the goals; too late to see Christian Eriksen's lashed half-volley that put Denmark in front; too late to watch Mile Jedinak's big-bearded sweating face gurning at the stands after levelling from the penalty spot; too late, thankfully, for the lengthy VAR delay that preceded it. Instead you watch these in slow-motion and from multiple angles, in between the soundless half-time images of pundits, and presenter. Though it spares you the empty talk of ex-pros, the lack of audio also means the high tempo of the second half is dulled; played out instead to a background of melodic pop muzak and the hushed chatter of the group of older men in short sleeve shirts having a low-key reunion around the big table behind you.

France 1-0 Peru

On the Golden Lane Estate evidence of the World Cup is sparing; a Colombian flag tacked to ninth storey glass and the thin white line with red centre of a St. George's cross blown back onto the balcony from which it was hung. The thwack of a tennis ball being hit back and forth echoes between the flats, the sun glints off high-rise windows, there's the growl of city traffic and somewhere nearby someone is drilling.

At Whitecross Street Market, the traders are piling up their rubbish on the corner of Roscoe Street, loading the last facets of their stalls into the back of battered transit vans, and offering their final wares to the baristas at Fix; each of whom wear a uniform of round-rimmed glasses. As you wait for an ice coffee you see a former colleague and stumble through a conversation script. What you're doing there. Where you went. Who's still there. Who you've seen. How things are. Surface level chat to fill no more than five minutes. Good to see you. You better be off. You may see each other again. You may not.

On Old Street, the smart shirts and trousers of silicon roundabout and the city's fringes quickly give way to the rolled-sleeve floral shirts and denim shorts of Shoreditch. In a barbershop window a big man with tattoo sleeves strokes his beard in contemplation, before commencing work on the facial hair of his doppelgänger. A family wheels an assortment of suitcases along the pavement, dad shielding the bright sunlight from his phone to consult directions.

"It's France against... Peraguay I think," says a man peering in the window of a bar on the corner of Shoreditch High Street and taking a punt based on the FRA and PER of the onscreen graphic. You press on a little further, to where a moderate hen party stands either side of the doors to Bar Kick. You squeeze past them and into the darkness of the pub; your eyes gradually adjusting to the gloom to take in a ceiling decked in the flags of the competing nations and walls crammed with football paraphernalia that fills every bit of plaster between television screens and floor.

Not wanting to spoil anyone's view you lean against a cabinet on the far wall between the bar and waiting staff busy waiting. Their colleagues arrive for the evening shift and are given hugs of a sincerity greater than those with which you greet your family after months apart. Though you came with the intention of supporting the underdog, your end of the bar is emphatically French. Shirts spanning the last two decades of Les Bleus adorn attractive young metropolitans, and it's hard not to get swept up in the cacophony of noise and excitement – loud roars bereft of consonants – that soundtrack any approach on the Peruvian penalty area. When Kylian Mbappe taps France in front, arms and flags are aloft long before ball meets net.

There is, it transpires, a Gallic majority in personnel not just in front of the bar, but behind it too and so come half-time the on-screen analysis is muted in favour of a fifteen minute blast of French language pop. The beats of Jacques Dutronc bringing joyous smiles, the occasional clap or a shake of the hips, from those coming back into the gloom from interval cigarettes; hand-painted tricolours on cheeks, 'Zidane 10' on their backs.

The second-half offers a stool at the bar and a better view and though you still crave a Peruvian equaliser – finding yourself leaping out of your seat when Pedro Aquino thwacks a thunderbolt off the bar – it's hard not to be pulled into the joy de vivre of the French crowd around you. Smiling and joking and singing, occasionally dancing; they're living the World Cup, and the moment and the city, whilst you merely sit on the periphery. You place your empty beer bottle on the bar, and step, blinking, back into the early evening light.

Argentina 0-3 Croatia

You miss this game. It's on your television, and you're sitting in front of it, but you don't take it in. The shock result of the tournament and you will remember nothing of it beyond Ante Rebic's thumping volley; the sudden burst of noise from crowd and commentary briefly heaving you back into your surroundings to register the sight of his hands-on-ears victory trot. But the afternoon beer and your seat on the edge of others' enjoyment has left you with a morose feeling you can't shrug off. Your vision blurs and your focus drifts and the light gradually fades again.

Brazil 2-0 Costa Rica

In the office the talk is of last night's game. Ordinarily the talk is never of last night's game. Not in the fourteen months you've been here has the talk been of last night's game. But a traditional big name beaten by a lesser-known opponent is noticed by those whose interest in football would lay dormant in any other year. Your opinion is sought. "Aye, Rebic's goal was some finish." What else can you say?

It's a quiet summer Friday, bereft of deadlines and pressure, and bursts of chatter extend the length of the open office space. There is laughter next to you, and you join a trio of colleagues crowding round a monitor where, over in St. Petersburg, Neymar is making the most of a foul. You scoff along with the others as he hams up his dramatic slow-motion backwards tumble like a man falling into a pool in an Ealing comedy.

"You'd be embarrassed to be of the same nationality," says one colleague, before another shushes him and gestures to the Brazilian designer who sits on the next bank of desks, working silently in the headphones he wears from 9am to 5pm each day.

Nigeria 2-0 Iceland

"Nigeria have just scored," says a guy in a high-vis vest and cement spattered trousers, sitting uncomfortably on a bike rack on Central Street. His mate stands eight feet away on the kerbside smoking a cigarette, but he doesn't acknowledge him. Instead he continues to look up the street, agitatedly kicking together the heels of his hefty work boots.

You pass between them, along a footpath scattered with errant items which have escaped the clothes banks outside the prefab children's nursery, before pausing on the bench outside Finsbury Leisure Centre. As you scroll back through the live footage on your phone, a dozen lads in England shirts, an equal number of white and red, file through a gate and onto one of the five-a-side pitches.

You find the Nigerian goal just as another of the players from your regular game arrives. You beckon him over and the two of you huddle over your screen to block out the light. As Ahmed Musa's volley tests the tethering of the Icelandic net you both draw breath; what a finish. As you turn to enter the building a wayward shot cannons off the fence behind you with a metallic crash.

Serbia 1-2 Switzerland

The Trader is much quieter than it had been for last Friday's Iberian altercation, enabling six of you to commandeer a table beneath the big screen. The guy behind the bar wears a Nigeria shirt and you kick-off a conversation by asking who scored their second goal. Able to open a chat with a stranger without the usual anxiety; comforted by familiar surroundings, familiar people, a familiar topic. You wanted Nigeria to win, you tell him, but purely so their group is blown wide open. He is part Nigerian, but only bought the shirt because he liked it. It's a good shirt. The guest ale is off again. Always is. He better just serve this lady.

You sit and watch the late evening game purely for moments of quality, moments of interest; collectively critiquing the performances as if it were they who were clumsily plundering through a Friday night seven-a-side game, and you who were the cream of your nation's footballing talents.

"I'd have put that away."

"He needs to be squaring that."

"He's got to get over the ball."

Granit Xhaka levels things up for Switzerland, prompting a

lively debate about what should be expected of the Serbian goalkeeper.

"Let's not fall out over the merits of Swiss equaliser."

"Aye, it's not what the Swiss would've wanted."

You're reminded of the time the CEO disappointedly pulled out Switzerland in your sweepstake for the last World Cup, and how – on that, your first interaction with him – you'd tried to console him with a joke. The retelling of the punchline is interrupted as your collective reaction to Xherdan Shaqiri curling a shot against the post startles a woman exiting the ladies toilets.

And then Shaqiri is breaking clear, and your shouts prompt the rest of the pub to look to the screen as he bears down on goal and slots the ball home. He gives the Albanian Eagle symbol, he takes off his shirt, he stands and flexes angrily in the Kaliningrad drizzle.

"What would be your celebration?" asks a face turning away from the slow-motion replay of the Swiss forward's surprisingly pale torso.

"I reckon I'd Klinsmann it."

"Shirt off... maybe even the shorts if it's the last minute."

"I'd be over to the bench for a pile-on."

"I'd be in the crowd. I'd take the booking... even if I already had one."

Thirty-five years old, still dreaming of a World Cup goal.

You bid your farewells, sling your bag over your shoulder and head off down Whitecross Street. Cabbies return to their vehicles from their Friday night fish and chips at Kennedy's, joking about missed fares and food consumption. Teenagers loiter on the market tables outside Waitrose, the sound of cutlery on crockery carries from the tapas place, a chef takes a cigarette break by a side door. A bouncer outside The Jugged Hare sighs and looks to his watch.

Golden sunlight reflects off high-rise windows, highlighting the last of the evening drinkers on the Barbican waterside. On Milk Street three young women on severe heels totter tentatively towards a bar they don't know. Outside Bow Wine Vaults city types play out the same old arguments about who should get the bill; you step between stacked cardboard and pavement drinkers and fist-bump the statue of the Cordwainer on Watling Street, his knuckles shining from all those who do as you do.

In Bloomberg Arcade a man in a sling tries to photograph his meal whilst his female companion smokes away the last of her cigarette. You pause as a cyclist runs a red light, drop sixty-seven pence in the paper cup of the man in the sleeping bag outside Cannon Street. Trip up the top step, make a light jog through the barriers, board a train that rolls off into the pinking evening sky; catching sight of a plane banking between the tops of the skyscrapers towards City Airport, fuselage turned fuchsia by the late evening sun.

Belgium 5-2 Tunisia

It's hot and bright. London is a city of bare legs; shorts and summer dresses. Tourists and day-trippers fill the pavements of

The Strand and the cobbles around Covent Garden Market. On the fringes of the market square, people queue and wait in the shade for late brunches and early lunches; holding out for an outdoor spot at which to be both seated and seen. International waitresses and waiters glide between tables; cigarette smoke mixes with the smells of al fresco dining. Beyond the restaurants and flagship stores, people in sunglasses peer at maps on street signs, and stand idly in the way of side roads.

On Drury Lane, Lowlander Grand Cafe is full and you don't have a reservation.

"Everyone is Belgian, they're here for the football," says a well-dressed man at a plinth by the door.

"Yeah, that's why I'm here."

You pause for a moment, contemplating your next move, but also in the faint hope he may've perhaps overlooked a vacant seat. Magically the latter bears out, and you pick your way between tables and chairs. A bar packed with Belgians, yet you end up wedged in next to two southern wideboys; identifiable as English by being the only people in the building to have worn the novelty elephant hats, given away with Delirium, for longer than the duration of a token selfie. They rattle through intense Belgian beers as if they are cheap supermarket lager and are on their fourth by half-time.

The Lambic you've carefully chosen is yet to arrive when a table-top drum roll is followed by arms thrown aloft throughout the room; Eden Hazard's successful penalty draws a huge cheer inside and pulls inquisitive faces to the open doors and windows. Orders are made in English, all other conversation is conducted in French and Dutch, bowls of moules are ferried to tables of exiles craving a stronger taste of home. Cheeks are

55

streaked with waxy bars of red, black and gold, Red Devils scarves wrapped tightly round necks despite the heat; well dressed women sink pints.

At half-time, the background drone of punditry on an unassailable Belgian lead inexplicably pauses to make way for a football-themed song from a children's cartoon. One by one the excited conversations fade out and, led by a man on the mezzanine balcony head-banging away in Belgium shirt and elephant hat, the entire cafe claps along to the techno beat of *'Kicky Kicky Kick Kick'*. The song ends, there's a few seconds of laughter, and the conversation fades up again as if the last two minutes were merely a trip. Behind you a waitress returns from the kitchen and her colleagues try to convince her what just happened, just happened.

South Korea 1-2 Mexico

Carrying a disappointing chain store rice dish, you find a vacant bench between the pigeons of Victoria Embankment Gardens upon which to eat. On the next seat along a Canadian tourist is explaining the London Eye to a friend. "It's like a slow-assed Ferris wheel ride, but with strangers." Accurate, but probably not one for the posters.

As you approach Charing Cross, you meet Anti-Brexit protesters peeling away from their march route. Placards are carried over shoulders; European flags tied around shoulders or waists, bright yellow 'Bollocks to Brexit' stickers stand out on their t-shirts and sun hats like cat's eyes. Point made, they assimilate back into the weekend. In Trafalgar Square a celebration of Eid is taking place, a bright pink stage facing a crowd dotted with hijabs and raised arms. In the surrounding streets daytime drinkers spill onto the pavements outside dark old pubs.

On Northumberland Avenue, the metal and glass of the Korean Cultural Centre stands out against its Georgian neighbours. It's gone kick-off when you muster enough bravery to try the door. A polite woman at a trestle table welcomes you in, tells you the basement is full but you can watch the match in this reception area. You sit, but it's soon clear the time difference between Rostov-on-Don and London is around seven seconds shorter downstairs than up. The excited noise beneath your feet letting you know how attacks have panned out down in the basement before they've got going here on the ground floor.

It was something your cognitive behavioural therapist had said that brought you here. Something that stood out to you between the worksheets and poorly sketched diagrams in that small green room. She'd talked up the merits of situations where you and everyone else present are invested in the same thing. So you feel part of something rather than isolated and alone. And you've long had enough of feeling alone. So you've chosen to seek out Belgians, and Koreans, and later Swedes, just as you sought Colombians, Poles and Egyptians earlier in the week. An attempt to find company through atmospheric osmosis. You've made it this far. And so, after ten minutes psyching yourself up, you edge away from isolation and down the steps to the basement.

You pull the curtain aside to be met by around one hundred and fifty pairs of concentrated eyes looking just over your right shoulder. Wedged between stark concrete walls and bookcases, on any available seat or bench are Koreans and the occasional Korean sympathiser. You squeeze down the side of the room, and dissolve into a back corner. Between you and the screen, shirts are almost exclusively red; cheeks host temporary Korean flag tattoos, inflatable 'Fighting Korea' noise makers are thundered together over heads; a man beats a drum. Everyone is enraptured by the action, with the exception of one elderly woman, who sits at a table at the back of the room, somehow unfazed by it all as she reads a Korean book on gardening from the library shelves.

The broadcast is in Korean, but such is the noise whenever Korea so much as touch the ball in Mexico's half the commentary is rarely heard. Carlos Vela's penalty for Mexico brings the mood down, but not for long. Screams, shouts and a thudding of percussion echo in the space; it's a deafening din. You feel the sweat dripping off you, and are handed a free bottle of water by a centre volunteer; they offer you a can of Efes as a chaser, but you politely decline. The company is comfort enough.

Whilst the city above your heads will have greeted Son Heung-Min's consolation with the temperance an unimportant, albeit spectacular, goal merits – down here all context is gleefully ignored. Everyone is on their feet; screaming, cheering, applauding, hugging, drum-beating, smiling. It's too little too late, but it's a fleeting extension of home at least.

58

Germany 2-1 Sweden

On the fringes of Chinatown a drunk middle-aged man is having a very one-sided argument with a bouncer; his voice carrying above the dance beats of breakdancing buskers on nearby Leicester Square. "You're a fucking disgrace, you'll be sacked tomorrow, wait 'til Big Ian hears... I tell you!"

On the corner of Lisle Street and Newport Place, Ku Bar has a sign in the window boasting its cocktail lounge to be a 'football free zone'. The doorman laughs and jokes with two guys in vest and shorts. A young man with an incredibly sun-burnt face sips on a long drink. Men pile up cardboard boxes on the street edges opposite restaurants. You nip in the Chinatown Bakery, drawn in by the sweet smell that takes you back to a trip to Hong Kong and trying to explore a city on a budget.

In Soho Square you're gifted an empty seat by a departing family and unpack your rolls from their individual paper bags. The benches and grass of the small park are packed with socialising bodies. Shiny '2' and '8' balloons bob above a dozen pairs of lounging legs, the opening refrain of *'Don't Worry Be Happy'* carries across the grass from a portable speaker. An old man takes on all-comers at table tennis and the smell of weed hangs heavy and peacefully above heads.

You descend the stairs into Nordic Bar; and can feel the heat of the people already packed inside the moment you step through the door. The bar is three deep, the space a mismatch of Swedish expats, friends, and day-long day-out drinkers in loud shirts and slip-on shoes. You wedge yourself into a spot by the narrow bar that just about affords you a view between heads and flags. You look at the small rectangular representations of

59

Kyrgyzstan, Qatar, Ethiopia and Togo flapping in the breeze of the air-con and marvel at the gumption of whoever sold the bar this bunting.

The match is hard to follow in the bustle and jostle and a need to be on tip-toes whenever a meaningful attack unfolds. A man and woman try to eat a huge pile of chicken wings without a surface on which to rest the tray; two tiny women rely on their taller friends for a running commentary. Ola Toivonen's opening goal brings a light drizzle of beer and cocktails as arms struggle to celebrate in the throng.

The crowd thins a little for the second-half; people leaving as they value a vantage point over patriotism. A stag do commences an ill-timed game of beer pong in the tiny corridor space behind you. Their laddish cheers contradict the match action, leaving much of the clientele anxious that the screen they're watching is not showing the same events as others elsewhere in the pub. Between ping-pong balls ricocheting off your calves and insufferably loud banter a drunk Swede, undaunted by Marco Reus' equaliser, spends the second-half intermittently singing "Deutschland's going home" in the direction of a couple of distant German national shirts.

Then, right at the end, as it seems all is lost. A free-kick. A final chance. For the first time since you got here, a hush descends; glasses are clutched under chins, all eyes are on the screen. Toni Kroos swings his right boot, Robin Olsen swings a desperate left paw, heads swing to the far post, where the ball swings into the bright white nylon of the net. A few isolated pockets of celebratory noise dot around the pub. An audible "Fuck!" or three. Deutschland isn't going home. Not yet.

Outside, you climb the metal steps and turn left along the pavement. And as you do so you're hit by an immense sadness that falls over you like the shadow of the first cloud on an otherwise sunny day and runs through you from head to toe. What now? What now there's no-one else to surround yourself with? No-one to pretend you've a connection to? It's just you, and the darkening skies, and one less day of the weekend to hide in. Your stride shortens, your pace lessens; you watch the reflection of street-lamps roll over the windscreen of a double-decker bus, and you pick your way across Oxford Street and back towards the river; another Saturday night in the city blurring away around you impenetrably.

England 6-1 Panama

7.30am on a summer Sunday in Deptford. In the Caribbean cafe-bar where Deptford Broadway becomes New Cross Road – the one that spends its weekdays hidden behind shutters, and the constant high-pitched whine of an ancient burglar alarm – Saturday is only just coming to an end. In between stacked chairs, older men lean against tables, shirts undone to the waist, jewellery resting on moist chests; a woman in animal print totters carefully through the door, another asks for directions to a taxi rank.

On the High Street, men in Lycra and beards stand astride expensive cycles, making idle chat as they wait for their grand depart from the pavement outside London Velo. In a half-open second floor window above The Orient restaurant, a woman carefully applies eye make-up in a mirror placed on the ledge. A man unlocks the door to the nameless off-licence beneath a sign for Worldwide Money Transfer, another kneels to stack shelves inside the Chinese supermarket. The white-coated young men at M.Y. Butchers Cash & Carry are setting out their stall, wheeling out fruit and veg from beneath wonky awnings; huge yams piled up like fire logs beside an Alpine hut.

A plane streaks a stark white dividing line across the bright blue sky. The driver of a bin lorry leaves his truck idling as he nips down Comet Street for a mid-shift cigarette. A woman with a pram puts an index finger to the glass as she inspects the small ads in the window of Kim's Newsagents; at the solitary table outside Cafe Bianca an older guy sits alone with a styrofoam cup of coffee. As he lifts the cup to his mouth the shadow of another man steps out from Hales Street; the low morning sun ensuring it emerges from between the buildings seconds before its owner.

You haven't slept a wink. When daylight started seeping through the curtains, and you began to hear the intermittent hum of Heathrow-bound planes high overhead, you gave up trying. That's why you're up at this hour. Walking to save staring at the same walls, the same screens. You'll go on, right through Deptford, through the estates and the cranes and the hoardings, you'll take a bus to Bermondsey, an Overground to Haggerston, and a wander through Hoxton to the streets of Finsbury, going nowhere in particular but looking up as you do, to spy the flags that hang from balconies and windows. Portugal, Brazil, Spain and Poland; Colombia, France and England – shows of patriotism from on high.

By the time you turn to head to Old Street station and make your way back south of the river, people who've risen at a more reasonable hour are beginning to gather for the match. Six lads laugh and joke through the door of The Masque Haunt, four of them wearing England shirts of a vintage older than they; the red nineteen of Gascoigne the last to cross the threshold. At Old Street roundabout and onto the Tube the frequency of England shirts increases, white nylon torsos among the tourists and the couples ferrying foliage back from Columbia Road market.

Ninety minutes later, at a bus stop opposite the cemetery on Brockley Road, an old woman is talking to you about the weather ("it's no good at all for my plants"), the irregular bus service ("they say they're supposed to be every eight to ten minutes, but I don't know"), and the dog being walked on the opposite side of the street ("it lives two doors down from me that dog"). Without her glasses, she asks you to read out the numbers of any approaching buses, and as you do, she proceeds to tell you about her own dog's imminent death from cancer.

The reason you're standing here, trying to find the right facial expression to react to the slow tragic decay of a stranger's pet, is that you foresaw the imminent England-Panama kick-off as an opportune time for a haircut. It was not. Rather than settling into sofa or pub as you presumed, South London's male population are in your barbers. You could see the seats packed with waiting figures through the barbers' window as you crossed the road, but you couldn't turn on your heels. You'd have been embarrassed. Someone would have seen you. You'd have looked stupid. So instead you chose to walk on, out of your way, and now here you are; standing at a roadside calling out numbers whilst a woman lists symptoms of dog borne cancer. You're conducting the grimmest cup draw in the world.

By kick-off you're back on what passes for your sofa, but the commentary and punditry is already grating. Perhaps it's the abundant undisguised partisanship, perhaps it's just the lack of sleep. You move a few cushions around, lie down to get comfortable, and somewhere between the anthems and the opening goal, you drift away... until Guy Mowbray yells to startle you awake. A pattern emerges; your concentration dilutes and fades, your eyes close, you sleep, only to be woken by another England goal. As Jesse Lingard celebrates in slow-motion you fumble for the remote control and cut your losses. Time, at last, for bed.

Japan 2-2 Senegal

From your blurry slumber you're roused by the whir of vibrating metal on wood. Face in pillow, you fumble blindly at the bedside table and then turn your head to slowly focus on a message. It's an invite to the park, albeit from over an hour ago, that has only just buzzed through. You reply apologetically and raise yourself, shuffling to the living room, stumbling to the sort-of-sofa just in time for the second half. Men in all blue and all white moving purposefully with an energy at odds with your own.

The phone buzzes again, the invite to the park has evolved to an invite to the pub at the end of the road, and you know it's a friendly, well-meaning nudge to ensure you don't spend the day at home alone, again. So you take it as intended and reply with acceptance, find some clothes, splosh some water on your face, run some wax through your hair, pause to watch Takashi Inui's curling chip glance off the top of the crossbar, turn off the television and head for the door.

Poland 0-3 Colombia

The barman of the Ladywell Tavern apologises for your pint being the best part of six quid. It's good beer so you take the hit and step back outside for a table on the street. Your back to the sun, you put down the glass, and push the used ashtray to the table's furthest end. The street is busy as always; faces gawp out from passing buses, people go in the respective doors of the two newsagents across the street, re-emerging shortly after with ice-lollies or cold drinks.

Your friend arrives, and via a trip to the bar takes a seat opposite; she shuffles her position so the shadow of your head shields her sunglass-covered eyes from the sun, until it finally drops behind a tree up the street, allowing her to stretch out. An old friend of the flat-mate of your former girlfriend, this has never been a close friendship, but you talk openly and sympathetically and you realise that, aside from your sessions in therapy and counselling, this is the first genuine face-to-face conversation you've had with someone in a month. Possibly longer. How did it get to this?

On the television in the corner, blue shirted men are celebrating as you drop your glasses on the bar. The air is cooling now, and your friend pulls on a jumper for the walk home. You hug at the top of your road and head your respective ways; you jogging across the street before the traffic lights return to green. Back home, enlivened, or at least encouraged to be you for a little longer, you sit down to the second half. Your renewed enthusiasm leading you to applaud James Rodriguez' pass for Colombia's third goal. And you'll go to bed at least able to rise again.

USA 1994

Eleven-years-old, well and truly hooked on football; a summer spent telling anyone and everyone that Wales had gone closer than England had to being part of all this. Those American kits, the bags of water, the dishes of the parabolic microphones, the men on the touchline in pale blue suits and bright yellow caps. In your kickabouts – in the goals left standing on St. Michael's School field, or between jumpers down the Welfare – you were Roberto Baggio or Gheorghe Hagi, you celebrated goals on parched Doncastrian grass with Bebeto's cradle rock, or Finidi George's dog walk.

Yet, bar the odd moment beamed into your living room in that distinctive sun-faded colour of American broadcasts – Ray Houghton's forward roll, John Aldridge's jabbing finger, Iordan Letchkov flying through the air – USA '94 seemed to happen largely while you were sleeping. Rushing down in the morning, rewinding the VCR, and trying to watch as much of the previous night's highlights as possible before being shouted to the car to head to school. Rewinding and rewatching Saeed Al-Owairan's mazy dribble as your cereal went soggy.

The latter stages of that tournament faded away. You remember nothing of the semi-finals. By that point in the summer your parents' night-time arguments had become more frequent. You can't remember when they started, just the smash of a glass downstairs one night. You'd been watching the late film in bed, sound turned down on the small colour television. Stakeout it was, Emilio Estevez forever associated with your sister and you emerging from your rooms to exchange glances on the landing.

By the time of the final your dad had gone to spend time at your grandparents. A holiday without you. Or so you thought at the time. Being coerced downstairs by your mum to watch an empty game in an empty living room. Not knowing how to feel as the final spot-kick kept on rising and Roberto Baggio watched its unending trajectory before bowing his head to look to the turf.

Uruguay 3-0 Russia / Saudi Arabia 2-1 Egypt

A dead Monday for dead rubbers. You've made it out of your bed and out of your door, and that feels like a victory. Still, you're yet to get over the weekend's disrupted sleep, and so you do all you can to spend your day inside yourself. Headphones in, you speak only to decline the offer of hot drinks, and you follow the matches in a corner of your laptop screen silently, without reaction. They don't matter, you don't matter. Your body is here; present enough for a head count. That will do.

Iran 1-1 Portugal / Spain 2-2 Morocco

London is melting. The temperature has edged past thirty degrees. You wore shorts to work. The Southbank Centre's Riverside Terrace is a juxtaposed tableau of graduates in heavy gowns and mortarboards jutting against swimsuited children splashing and screaming in the fountain. Along the South Bank sweat drips off evening joggers and you catch your reflection in the sunglasses of the people passing you by. Doors to coffee shops and cafes are left open, releasing the whir of their blenders as they crush the ice of another frappe. Down by The Anchor couples and their drinks rest along the length of the riverside wall, enjoying the shade offered by the office blocks of Southwark Bridge Road. Women in Lycra stride purposefully towards post-work workouts.

In Downside Fisher Youth Club you congregate once again

under the small television in the corner, though there is less of an audience for the run through of Iran's line-up than there had been for England's opening game a week earlier. You shake hands and exchange hellos with arriving friends and reply to the 'be there in 5' and 'sorry work is mental at the moment' WhatsApps of those still on their way.

"What does the IR before Iran stand for?" asks one of your group as you turn to head up the stairs to the sauna-like sports hall, and you have him believing "In red" until the very last flight.

An hour later you're squeezed round a table in The Draft House on Tower Bridge Road; the three of you whose football interest is more than biannual, lamenting the pub's decision to screen Spain-Morocco over the more pivotal Iran-Portugal match. An errant shot at goal offers explanation; the regular Monday night clientele of sweaty post-dodgeball teams, office catch-ups and dating couples, tonight includes a table of Spaniards, hunkered expectantly beneath the corner television.

Morocco rattle the woodwork and one of the men on the Spanish table yells out in both anger and relief.

"What is it with Spanish people and shouting at the television?" asks one of your friends, adding, "my housemate does it."

A conversation ensues in which you determine the common denominator to be not the nationality of the television watchers, more so the football they are watching.

"Well I enjoy *Game of Thrones*, but I don't yell at it," concludes the friend.

Your group thins; people up and leave for trains and Tubes, bicycles and buses, to return to their own corners of the city.

69

Only two of you hang back long enough to join in with the cheers for Youssef En-Nesyri's bullet header that gives Morocco the lead. Across the pub the same Spanish man shouts another obscenity, before putting his face in his hands.

Interest throughout the room rises; more pairs of eyes fix on the television screens. Disparate groups with distant lives united by a common purpose; the potential for Spanish disappointment. You fade back to conversation for a moment, only to be jolted out of it by a loud shout of "Vamos!" and thunderous two-person applause. Iago Aspas has flicked in an equaliser. The cheers are quickly halted by a referral to VAR. The screen is split into three; replays of the goal, the referee with his head in a monitor, whatever is happening between Iran and Portugal. There is no sound on the television, no commentary. No-one knows what's going on and the pub is now a chatter of strangers conferring group permutations. Social barriers broken down by discussions over goal difference. Just as your friend is discussing the value of head-to-head records with a New Zealander seated three tables away the screen suddenly cuts to celebrating Spaniards. The pub's Spanish contingent are on their feet too. They've survived. They've progressed. Just.

Denmark 0-0 France / Australia 0-2 Peru

You should be in work. Instead you are squeezing out of a packed Tube train at Edgware Road and into the enveloping warmth of another day of a London heatwave. You woke up wishing you didn't exist. You just couldn't do it. Couldn't face it, couldn't see a way through it. You weren't suicidal. That would be painful; irresponsible even; awkward for all involved. You just felt everything would probably be much easier if you ceased to be.

Outside the station entrance people poke straws at the melting ice of takeaway coffees. A woman who has been sleeping rough in the rear doorway of an office complex perches on the kerbside with a bottle of water, washing her hands and arms above a drain. Clive Tyldesley's voice carries from Merchant Square; the match has already kicked off. Played out on a big screen as people lounge on the grass below; some smugly in deckchairs, others propped up on elbows. A couple of French shirts; 'Zidane 10', a more recent training top, a touch of face paint, but this is largely a neutral crowd for largely a neutral match. Smokers stepping out from office side doors give events a cigarette's worth of their time, but nothing more. Thirty feet up, people at desks stretch in their chairs, leaning back to glance out through the glass, check the score and people watch.

Down here on the turf, the number of more smartly attired football watchers gradually increases. People who've negotiated an early finish, ducking, so as not to impede the views of those already lounging, as they fill the gaps on the yellowing-green and try to get comfortable. Children already collected from school and daycare run and play between the faces that look up at the screen waiting for something, anything to happen. But beyond the occasional cutaways to a much better game, it never does. 'A summer of fun', it says on either side of the screen, but France and Denmark can't see that from Russia. A man cycling past takes a break to readjust his attire. "Jeez! Still nil-nil?" he says, before putting his sunglasses on and continuing off round the basin.

Half an hour later, on the Paddington arm of the Grand Union Canal two men in adjacent boats are discussing the permutations of the earlier results. The one on the boat nearest the bank pushes his sunglasses to his forehead to focus more intently on the screen of his mobile phone. "So yeah, it's France and Denmark that go through," he says, in an unexpectedly broad Yorkshire accent.

Further along the waterway you chance upon the opening exchanges of an argument between two men, one on a bicycle, the other walking on the supposedly bicycle-free towpath. It's getting unnecessarily heated, threats are being made. You can't pass by them, it's too late to turn away, so you chance the weight of your innocence and step between them. You usher both men apart with sympathetic tones you don't mean. Clearly angry at more in life than being asked to dismount for a few yards, the man on the bike shuffles backwards a few steps before screaming "Fuck you and fuck the sign!" He remounts and cycles off, wobbling angrily past a small child devouring a Calippo, whose mother covers his ears. The pedestrian thanks you. You just want a quiet life.

Nigeria 1-2 Argentina / Iceland 1-2 Croatia

Among the high-rises of the Warwick Estate a woman on a tenth floor balcony stubs her cigarette out in a flower-pot and retreats back inside. Flags of Portugal and Colombia hang from the balconies of her neighbours; though more prominent in position, they are lesser in number than the St. George's crosses that obscure ground-level windows and doors on the surrounding streets. Cycle-bells ding from the towpath, the siren of a fire engine blares by, and from the playgrounds behind Edward Wilson Primary School, carries the screams and yells of children.

Back at Paddington Basin, the offices have turned their workforce out into the sunshine; lanyards swapped for sunglasses as people pack the terraces and outdoor spaces of bars and cafes. You pick your way around them, from The Westway to the water's end; a solo figure blending into the background of a mass of couples and groups, a sullen *Where's Wally*, only noticeable if you're really looking.

You can't drink, but head into the pub at the end of the basin to watch the first half.

"Can I have a lemonade?" you ask the person behind the bar.

"I don't know, can you?"

You're not in the right frame of mind for such quirkiness, the assumption that you are frustrates you. You're tired, you're sad. So you just stand awkwardly until she finally decides you can and goes off to find a glass. You're not a regular, you don't know her, and now you feel like a prick for not being socially adept enough for what should've been a simple interaction.

You sit uneasily by the window, on the bar's periphery, still feeling awkward. You're unable to shake the feeling you're being judged by the bar-staff and subsequently by anyone they interact with. 'See that guy over there, he didn't join in my banter about whether he could have a drink or not, he just wanted a drink, weirdo.' Any sound of laughter has you glancing over your shoulder to see if they are directed at you, to see if

73

anyone is looking your way. But then, at 7:14pm, just in front of the halfway line, Ever Banega looks up, spots a distant run, and pings a long right-footed pass perfectly into the path of a blurring movement of white and sky blue stripes.

The blur is Lionel Messi, and the ball lands on the '10' of his shorts like a dart in a bullseye. Despite the distance it has travelled, he deftly removes all its pace and cushions it effortlessly onto his left boot, barely breaking stride. This second touch pushes it perfectly into his path and as he shapes to shoot with his right foot, Francis Uzohu in the Nigerian goal seems to shrink under the weight of the Argentine's reputation; despite arms and legs outstretched his body contracts at the near-post like a spider going down a plughole. He has no chance. This is only going in. It's brilliant, and you can't help but smile, you may even have applauded. Messi sinks to his knees, looks up and points his index fingers to the sky. And just like that you're you again.

For half an hour anyway. That is until you step into another of those rooms on the corner of Little Venice, and your world and every waking thought and fear you have closes back down on top of you.

South Korea 2-0 Germany / Mexico 0-3 Sweden

For a second straight morning you've been unable to face the day, unable to gather the motivation to leave your bed, to fulfil sincerely made plans to be at your desk for 8.30am. Not sleeping, not groggy, just repeatedly prodding the snooze option because why not? The 7.30 train has left, the 7.45, the 7.50, the 8.17, the 8.47 and still you lie there. What's the point? At 9.30am you find the resolve to roll from the bed and send an email to say you'll be working from home. That in itself feels like success enough for one morning.

At lunchtime a fruitless stare into an empty fridge forces you to shower and dress and head out into the light. The grass at the end of the road has crumbled away to a yellowing dust; children hare around the playground of the primary school; small dogs yap at owners who won't throw balls for an eighteenth time. A loose screw means number 16 is halfway to becoming number 91. On your return, a fundraiser in an oversized red t-shirt stands looking up from the pavement, making her pitch to a man leaning from the window of the upstairs flat nextdoor. You nod a hello as you fumble for your keys and can hear the television of the man downstairs as you step through the door.

You flick on your own set, push open the windows, and adopt a horizontal position on the futon. The commentary competes with the whoosh and clack of passing trains, the occasional shouts of children carrying from the school, and the clattering whir of a distant drill, but the breeze is welcome and your interest only fleeting. Your empathy for the underdog enough to have you draw breath as Manuel Neuer fumbles a free-kick, but not enough to make you put down your phone.

But slowly, steadily, the second half gathers you in; a strong one handed save from Jo Hyeon-Woo hauls you up off your back; a neat Korean attack causes you to place your phone on the table. As Germany huff and puff in your living room, Sweden are finding their stride in Yekaterinburg. The coverage split-screens to a ball hitting the net and yellow-shirted arms in the air once, twice, three times, whilst Jonathan Pearce spends more time banging on about the narrative of it all than a friend who's spent four years writing a screenplay.

Injury-time – the television now on mute – you're shouting "the defender's played it!" to whoever may happen to be passing by beneath your window, before the referee turns from his pitchside monitor and points to the centre spot. You hear the man downstairs cheer along with you as the Korean players stream towards the touchline in celebration. Just a couple of minutes later, you both yell out in unison as Neuer is left stranded and Ju Se-Jong gives the ball a spectacular hoof towards the empty net. By the time Son Heung-Min catches up with it to turn it into the unguarded goal you're up on your feet. You smile, you even clap, you're a world away from where your day began.

Serbia 0-2 Brazil / Switzerland 2-2 Costa Rica

It's hot. Again. But there's enough of a breeze to rustle the leaves of trees and bushes and force an elderly man on Adelaide Road to pause from his steady shuffle and wipe the dust from his eyes. In the barbershop on Brockley Road there are no customers; two of the four regular barbers sit on the long bench by the window, laughing at a mobile phone.

"It's traditional Bulgarian music," the bigger one says on seeing you walk in, "and you dance to it like this."

He duly provides a demonstration that gives you a first

laugh in days, before taking a small bow and ushering you into his chair.

Highlights of South Korea-Germany play out on the television above the mirrors.

"Did you see the game?" you ask, trying to nod upwards without moving your head.

"Yes, yes," he replies. "I am very happy. I am Korean... Did you not know this? I am Turkish Korean... but you cannot tell. I had an operation on the eyes."

You wince. You know you should probably say something, but you know the guys in here. They're good, they're welcoming of everyone. And you don't need more anxiety, more tense pauses. Instead you give him the silent treatment for a while... enough to show you're not amused.

Once he has finished with the clippers, as he is nearing the end of his work, you give him another go. Who does he want to win the tournament?

"I am supporting Croatia, England and Russia."

"Why Russia?" you ask.

"Because of the girls, I like the girls... if any Russian girls see me and ask me if I am supporting Russia, then I am supporting Russia."

A bell tinkles and a man deposits his two young children in the shop whilst he nips two doors down to get cash. They stand by the window naming the flags on the bunting that hangs from mirror to door.

"Are you Turkish?" one of them asks the barber.

"Yes, but there is no flag for that."

Crossing back through Hilly Fields Park a young boy dribbles a luminous ball across your path. "Harry Kane! One nil!" he shouts as he chips it against a tree trunk. A woman in a sundress paces the grass outside the cafe loudly holding her end of a decidedly middle-class phone conversation. "Oh, did I tell you I know Tamara? ...I know, I know... no, from tennis... yes absolutely..." A couple call frantically after their dog, which, enticed by the smell of food, has diverged from its circuit of the basketball court to head instead for the outdoor tables of the cafe. A toddler giggles as it sniffs around her feet.

Back in your living room, back on the futon, windows still open. You look up at the television to see Neymar writhing on the floor, holding his ankle. You sigh and scroll the phone screen again; a glimpse at those you know who are out and about; on roof terraces, in beer gardens, up mountains, on beaches, smiling, happy, in groups. Together. You turn and look out the window; the sinking sun sends the shadows of the chimney pots and aerials from your side of the street creeping up the walls of the houses opposite. A rise in volume causes you to look back to the television; the ball nestles in the Serbian net, Paulinho is stumbling back to his feet. The game is over with seventy-five minutes left. Now what?

Senegal 0-1 Colombia / Japan 0-1 Poland

Eleven stories up, above the traffic of Elephant & Castle, a pair of bare arms smoke a cigarette from an open window. If they were to shield their eyes from the sun, the owner of these limbs would be able to see beyond the cranes and construction to the townhouses of Brixton, Clapham and Herne Hill. Look down and they'll see a queue of double-decker buses, and people too impatient for the green man breaking into a jog at the sound of a horn. And they'd see you, pointing to the bus stop for the woman who'd just asked you the way to New Cross, and above the noise of engines they might just catch the chords of the busker, whose butchering of *'Stand By Me'* is scattering the pigeons.

It's another hot, hot day. The sun beats down on the concrete and the staff of Castle Tandoori have propped open their door in an effort to entice in something approaching a breeze. Through it you can see glasses and cutlery neatly laid on proudly-white tablecloths, ready for guests yet to arrive. Once again the shopping centre is dotted with the yellow of Colombia shirts; they're visible on every concourse, in every shop, in every cafe.

Word has spread since the South Americans' opening game and Lost River Brewery now boasts two rooms of yellow-clad fervour. You step into the dark of the larger room just ahead of the anthems and find a spot that affords you as much of a view as you feel comfortable courting on what is very much someone else's day. Though you wouldn't know it from the sound of songs and horns that fill the steadily warming air, it's a drab first half – the only excitement coming as the referee uses VAR to overrule himself on a potential Senegalese penalty. You're not sure what the Spanish is for "See, I told you so," but you suspect you've just heard it in a chorus of two or three hundred voices.

"Who's next?" asks the barmaid, and you gesture to the middle-aged Colombian man to your right; yellow shirt fitting snugly over a spherical belly that offers a fine advert for decades

79

of compassionate home-cooking.

"Pint," he says.

"What of?"

He shrugs, "anything."

"Anything? I didn't think we were at that stage just yet," replies the barmaid with a smile before flipping the top of a lager tap.

Early in the second half you give up your vantage point to a trio of middle-aged Colombian women who are struggling to see, and perch instead behind a gaming machine. It's not a great spot but you've enough of a view to see Yerry Mina's header power up off the turf into the roof of the net, before the screen is lost to a blur of arms and a yellow mist of twirling scarves and billowing flags. People run out of the door and into the light, others hug, one is on top of the pool table; the bar staff laugh and shake their heads.

As injury-time ticks away, one man begins inching his way up the tallest of rigs upon which the ceiling is suspended. By the time the final whistle sounds he's more than fifteen feet up; punching the air with the arm that isn't clinging on tightly. Beneath him, flags are waved furiously in the stale air, horns are sounded, cowbells beaten, and the room flooded with the light from camera phones, as those present film the joyous throng for posterity, or for those not able to be part of it.

England 0-1 Belgium / Panama 1-2 Tunisia

Back in Lewisham a limousine is parked outside the flats at the bottom of Elmira Street. Beyond it, a sextet of young people dressed to the nines; two lads in suits and sunglasses, four teenage girls in dresses that shimmer in the early evening light. They stand against the wall, whilst an assembled paparazzi line of family members coo and compliment, and snap photos on phones and tablets.

You root around in the depths of your memory for recollections of your own school prom. A hotel – the name of which escapes you – across the other side of town. It was your school's first; commissioned when a joke suggestion, that may have been your own, got out of hand. 'Why stop at a party? Why not have a prom, like in the American films?' There wasn't even twenty of you sitting A-Levels, it wasn't that type of school; you had to rope in the entirety of Year 11 to make it viable. Almost half a lifetime ago now and all you can remember is walking into The Styrrup for a pre-minibus pint, dressed in the most reasonably-priced of Burton Menswear, and the barman greeting you with "court hearing lads?"

Back in the present, you've the taste of beer in you from the afternoon games and could go for another. You reason the Ladywell Tavern will have enough of a crowd for you to seem anonymous, yet not too big a one as to feel overwhelmed, and chance a walk to the end of the road for the second-half.

You choose to lean at the corner of the bar; a spot which offers you a sightline between oversized low-hanging lampshades to the television on the back wall, and also puts you in earshot of the young lads nursing soft drinks in the corner.

81

You've barely put pint glass to lips for a first sip when Adnan Januzaj rolls the ball out of his feet to curl an inevitable left foot shot into the top corner. Someone says "goal" the moment it leaves his foot, it may have even been you. The boys in the corner are not impressed.

"Ohhh. So shit so shit so shit."

"Oh my days. Oh my days."

"How're we doing?" asks a well-to-do woman in a bright orange dress, in from the beer garden and suddenly next to you at the bar. You decide to sidestep the assumption that you've a dog in this fight and tell her "England are 1-0 down."

"Typical," she replies, but you're not sure what of. A bar-wide chorus of groans causes you both to turn quickly back to the screen.

"These lot need to calm down fam, they need to calm down," is the advice from the corner.

"Danny Rose man, he needs to chill."

The woman heads back out to the garden, and her place is taken by another lady, one with a hefty handbag on her shoulder. She tells the barman she's here for a collection, and he asks her name before disappearing out the back of the bar. A few minutes later he returns with a well-wrapped whole crab. She thanks him, puts it in her bag and disappears out the door. Behind you the boys are in a debate.

"Ferdinand, Campbell, Terry, Woodgate. You can't put Stones in that bracket."

You suddenly have a lot of questions, but the inclusion of Jonathan Woodgate in a list of English defensive greats probably trumps the origin story of the crustacean.

As you ponder whether to pace your drinking to allow for a further pint, or just a half, Marcus Rashford breaks through on goal. All alone, seemingly destined to equalise. Yet somehow, just at the crucial moment, he forgets he's an international footballer and skews his shot horribly wide. Hands go to heads on the corner table. It doesn't look any better in slow motion.

"What even is that? What are you lot doing?"

"Look at that miss. All you have to do is bang it."

"Bang it in bro. Chip the keeper."

Full-time brings shaking heads and resigned looks across sullen tables. You hear the words "reality check" as you sup the last of your drink, put your glass on the bar, give a "thank you" to the barmaid and step outside. Another man follows with a hefty sigh, stopping at one of the street-side tables to ask a solitary smoker, "you got a lighter there bruv? I'm upset."

It's still warm, still light, and so you elect to take a long looping walk home. Up in Hilly Fields Park, a low golden light floods across the grass from above the rooftops of Montague Avenue and the spire of St. Andrew's. The setting sun is painting everything it touches with a warming ochre hue; the long parched grass, the Victorian bricks and slates of Prendergast School, the wood-panelled walls of the cafe. A couple stir from a blanket on the slope by the cricket field, a distant dog barks, a bird swoops silhouetted against the sky. You crest the park's summit and drop down into the shade of Vicars Hill, feeling a rare contentedness, ready to leave it all behind.

France 1998

Fifteen-years-old, rushing home from school, shirt untucked, sleeves rolled up, Tipp-Ex stained tie, excited for Scotland's opener with Brazil. Elaborate collages of the flags and kits of competing nations carefully drawn on your art folder. Sitting in the reception of the old British Coal building, waiting for a meeting about your work experience placement; listening to England-Tunisia on a portable radio. Catching the bus home afterwards and bumping into your sister on the top deck, her on her way back from a college exam.

A tournament watched almost exclusively in the living room of your mum's semi-detached. Getting in from school and turning on the television in time to see Jose Luis Chilavert's free-kick turned just over the bar; the back door wide open on a sunny weekend afternoon as Sunday Oliseh's wonder strike sank Spain. The hot bright Marseille sun blanching out the Argentina shirts to almost all white as Frank de Boer's pass sailed over them to be 'beautifully pulled down by Bergkamp!' Lying on the floor on a Sunday evening, cheering Croatia on against Germany; your mum trying to join in the excitement despite the two cats sleeping on her lap.

Shaun's parents away for the week and you and the older lot heading round there for England-Colombia – chants back and forth between the two sofas. Heading out into Doncaster after the game; your first night 'round town'. Bottles of Budweiser in The Coach & Horses, before heading on to Visage. Your hometown as you'd never seen it before; all shouts and screams and taxi lights and thudding music. High-

84

fives on the nightclub stairs after you made it in without an age check. Entering the office of your placement up on the sixth floor of the Council House the day after Argentina defeated England to be met by one of the graphic designers standing by the photocopier, shaking his head. "Bloody hell eh kid?"

The second round

France 4-3 Argentina

Two thirds of the way up Mynydd y Dref you find a man looking for a spot of earth supple enough to hammer in a windbreak. You exchange hellos and, as it ultimately proves the wind is too strong to be broken, you stumble into the opening exchanges of something approaching a conversation.

"When I was eighteen, I couldn't wait to get away from this place," he tells you. "Five years in London – Tooting and then Wood Green – and then I couldn't wait to get back here."

You stand side by side, looking out over a colour chart of blues; sea and sky broken only by the green wedge of Ynys Seiriol, and the tip of Y Gogarth's yellowing western slope. Empathy has never been easier to feel. You bid your goodbyes and go your separate ways; he descends into the Conwy valley defeated – poles and rolled up fabric on his shoulder – you head upwards, skirting the steep purple slopes to the summit.

You take in the views at the top and press on further. People dot along the sea-facing mountainside, clutching binoculars and long-lens cameras. The Red Arrows are scheduled over Llandudno, the mountain offering a prime, albeit distant, vantage point. Soon they come, roaring up the valley, thunder on a cloudless sky. Above the rooftops of Llandudno, they twist and turn, draw circles and hearts, and you take a seat on a rock to watch – but not for long. The weather hasn't been this good here since you were a child; best make the most of it. You cross the Sychnant Pass and take a path that winds around the slopes above The Fairy Glen, looking out across Dwygyfylchi and a hundred memories of simpler summers.

The high midday sun is glistening off the sea as you climb over stiles and tread rutted footpaths moulded into shape by the bike wheels and heavy boots of damper seasons, before being dusted a pale grey by the heatwave. You spend half an hour or more crossing fields, happily lost and alone in the freshness of the mountain-top breeze, before dropping down through the ferns and onto Sychnant Pass Road; walking the cool valley back into the town, and a self congratulatory stop-off for a quick one in The Albion. It's nice in there. Sociable and homely. You make it one and a half.

"Have you been enjoying the World Cup?" you'd asked your dad when you arrived, keenly anticipating a couple of days spent walking in the sun before sitting down with him for the matches.

"I've not really watched much of it," had been his reply and you had to try and hide your disappointment as he listed the not quite handful of games he had seen. You'd had to fill him in on which teams had made it to this stage and the matches scheduled for the weekend. France-Argentina was the pick you'd told him, but whatever its potential it could never pull him away from the bowling green on a summer Saturday afternoon. So you watch this alone too, as you have so many games up to now, save for occasional interruptions by the dog and your step-mum's head-in-the-door offerings of "a drink or anything?" and remarks on the ever increasing scoreline. "Four-three now? You said this would be a good one. Your dad will be sorry he missed it."

He won't be. He's spent his life watching football, and you know he'd much rather be on the touchline talking and joking with old friends and familiar faces at Penmaenmawr Phoenix than sitting here marvelling at the slow-motion replays of Benjamin Pavard's mesmerising, cutting, swerving, spinning half-volley. Hell, you would too.

Uruguay 2-1 Portugal

This morning wasn't your first walk in the fresh open air of North Wales. When you arrived on Friday afternoon, you barely set your bags down before heading off and out. Keen to take advantage of the good weather, of the sea air, and of the endless sky; the huge sheet of blue bereft of towers and planes and cranes. You set out along the coast path for the West Shore, all your anxieties and worries diffused by colours lifted straight off a child's painting, and the views -– out across the water, up into the hills and mountains, down onto the huge jellyfish beached on the sand. Relaxed and, for the first time in a long time, feeling something approaching contentedness. So much so you'd walked five miles to the very end of the Orme without even realising.

Now your body is feeling the effects of the sun and the long miles and the lunchtime beer and a half, and so you try to take advantage of the gap between games and attempt a nap. Lying on the bed, you listen to the noises; different to your own flat. No rattle of trains, no bi-minutely fly-by, instead it's a real quietness, punctuated only by the occasional squark of a seagull, the low hum of a car moving slowly down the road, or nextdoor's dog yapping through the walls.

"Watch these two passes," you say to your dad as he comes into the living room, drawn in by your reaction to Edinson Cavani's excellent opening goal. He nods his approval and takes a seat on the end of the sofa, before asking on sight of the third replay, "has he scored that with his face?" He stays there for the rest of the first-half, shaking his head and rolling his eyes as Ronaldo hitches up the legs of his shorts as if he's about to wade through a deep river in preparation for a free-kick that he'll eventually whack into the wall.

"Goal here," says your dad as Rodrigo Bentancur rolls the ball perfectly into the path of Cavani on the edge of the box, transporting you instantly back into your childhood. You were never sure whether his impeccable prediction of when a team on *Match of the Day* was about to score came from a lifetime spent in the game, or the fact he'd already read the goalscorers on Ceefax, or in the evening paper. Either way he never failed to get it right, and he doesn't now; Cavani wrapping his foot round the ball to curl it perfectly beyond the outstretched arms of Rui Patrício.

Spain 1-1 Russia

Two days of long walks and your dad's generous measures of late evening whisky have brought an inevitable lie-in. You wake to the delicate clicking of the blinds moving in the light breeze, and from beyond them the sound of a distant lawnmower and your dad having a one-way conversation with the dog. Breakfast is late and outdoors; cereal and instant coffee beneath another bright blue sky. A coating of suncream, and a walk round the dusty path that surrounds the estuary to Conwy. A coffee in the shade of a stone wall at the back of a cafe, as you watch families and tourists walk the castle walls.

Back at the house, the blinds are closed to prevent the continuing summer heatwave from blanching out the television screen. As they bend and roll in the draught from the open window you're offered glimpses of the scenery beyond; seagulls perched on the grey slates across the street and the greens and purples of the mountain you walked yesterday. You've barely found yourself a comfortable spot on the sofa when Spain take the lead; you and your dad laughing as the replay shows Sergei Ignashevich so busy fouling his man that he doesn't realise he's back-heeled the ball into his own net.

Russia draw level, but Spain's attempts to pass them into submission are failing, so too is your dad's alertness, as he begins to nod off in his favoured seat by the window. Chin dropping to chest, the occasional snore before he jolts his head back upright, eyes blinking. He sees little of extra-time, bar the moments in which you wake him with your reactions to saves and near misses. Just before the penalty shoot-out you nip to the toilet and through the open bathroom window you can hear Kevin Kilbane co-commentating in a house down the street.

You give muted reactions to each of the penalties, make uneducated guesses on whether the ball is about to meet net, or goalkeeper, or crowd. Nine kicks down, Iago Aspas has to score. The silent anticipation of Moscow, briefly reflected in a Deganwy living room. Igor Akinfeev goes too early, too far to his right, but somehow extends a foot and volleys the ball wide of the post. Among the replays, a camera shot from behind the bench. As the Russian substitutes and coaches leap in the air and surge forward, one man in a shirt and trousers turns to face the crowd. Bellowing into the evening sky, he punches his fists to the air alternatively, tie and accreditation flapping about wildly on his shaking torso. A purest of joy; an envious ecstasy.

Croatia 1-1 Denmark

"It's one-nil to Denmark already," says a lad at the table behind, just as the three of you are getting up to leave a Conwy pizza restaurant. You're a little disappointed to have missed kick-off, but for now you're mainly thankful to have survived the anxiousness of a meal-time worth of conversation. You can't remember when you began to find social conversation so hard, but it definitely flowed much easier when there were four of you, not three. You cross the road, into the shade of the castle walls and Croatia have equalised before you've even made it back to the car.

A little over fifteen minutes have gone when you make it to a television set, and then, nothing. As if the two nations had a pre-match agreement to go at it for the first quarter of an hour then hold out for penalties if things were all square. Less a football game, more a staring contest. On the match lumbers, like a video installation on the futility of man. You had in mind to go for a run at full time, and it seems to be the only way to ensure something might happen. Perhaps the two teams are just waiting for you to stop watching before they crack on again.

Your feet crunch on the gravel as you pass the last of the evening dog-walkers on the path around Conwy estuary. Boats list and birds pad about on the mud flats of low tide. The sun is setting as you run on toward Conwy harbour where people sit outside The Liverpool Arms or perch on the quayside wall to take in the last of the day's light.

The pink sky is closing in around a bright red dot of a sun – the sort that stays in your vision when you turn away, as if you've been staring at a lamp. The sound of The Proclaimers shuffles into your ears "It's over and done with, it's over and done with." Maybe it is. Maybe it finally is. You check the time, and the prospect of possible penalties spurs you to run rather than walk the final few hundred metres up the steep hill back to the house.

In through the back door, beyond the dog who greets you as he always does – as if you've been gone for a week and brought news of the demise of cats. With heavy breath and moistened brow you make it to the door of the living room in time for each side's respective fourth efforts.

"Two-two," says your dad, without looking up or back, "they've both missed one".

And once Lasse Schone's kick has been safely batted away by the palms of Danijel Subašić and the camera closes in on the Dane chewing his shirt in frustration, he asks, "were there many people out on the quay?"

Brazil 2-0 Mexico

You're somewhere just outside Crewe as Brazil and Mexico kick-off, sat in a windowless 'window seat' whilst the guy across the aisle ploughs through a huge bag of fried chicken at a steady unrelenting pace. Thankfully, as a trade off against the greasy darkness, the train's fierce air conditioning provides the most pleasant temperature your body has been exposed to in weeks.

An older couple unwrap tinfoil sandwiches from a cool-bag as they share a copy of *The Times*. A young man doesn't look up from a laptop. A man sleeps; his head against the window, reflected against itself – the frame of his spectacles, clacking off the glass as the train bumps and jolts. Phone signal rises and falls with the signs of life that blur past the window; backyards with washing lines and gazebos billowing in the breeze; greenhouse panes flashing in the mid-afternoon sun. It's one-nil as you get your first glimpse of a Tube train trundling along an adjacent line and the scenery begins to rise up around you, enclosing you again; the blue sky disappearing upwards beyond Victorian brick, post-war concrete and the glass and steel of now.

By the time you make it through a Euston station in the opening acts of rush hour to The Royal George, Brazil have scored a second goal. One of the many televisions that dot the bar is showing an aerial replay of the counterattack, yellow dots running at green ones. Just as you find a suitable leaning spot from which to watch the final minutes, there's the sound of glass smashing on pavement; the bar manager puts his palm to his forehead with a hefty sigh, the barman next to him merely shrugs and reaches for a broom.

In this half of the pub the clientele consists exclusively of solitary men looking towards wall-mounted screens. Men in suits, men in short sleeves, workmen in pocketed shorts and dust-covered shirts, decorators with white splatters across their work boots, and an all-out geezer; red polo-shirt, red shorts, deck shoes over sockless feet, phone glued to his ear above an indecipherable tattoo. A cheer from the saloon greets the final whistle and two yellow shirts blur noisily out the door; the bunting above the bar catches the breeze of a passing bus.

Belgium 3-2 Japan

On the grass of Potters Field Park the fixtures and fittings of a corporate pop-up are popping up or popping down, a midway state ringed by temporary fencing that pushes sun-chasers eastwards. Joggers stop and remove earphones, give head shakes and shrugs, confused by the semi-structure blocking their path. Couples attempt to line up selfies with the towers of Tower Bridge, well-to-do diners sit in sunglasses outside The Ivy. Among the people lounging on the scorched turf pigeons scavenge for crumbs of post-work snacks and late afternoon lunches, before the pop of a cork sends them scattering and sweeping off over the river.

Under the bridge and up the stone steps onto Tower Bridge Road. A late meeting is winding down in an office window, a middle-aged couple stand aghast outside the estate agents, slowly repeating sale prices to one another. You buy an overpriced sports drink from the tourist trap newsagents that sells snacks and snowglobes side by side, and take a shortcut down Queen Elizabeth Street, fresh flowers on the fence for the young lad stabbed there three years back.

"There's a downstairs?" asks a friend of The Draft House, a pub you've been coming in since the last World Cup. A big screen to yourselves; chairs and tables pulled from across the room and rearranged to suit the group dynamic of football watchers and non-watchers.

"He's hit it!" says a voice from the end of the row, the 'it' reaching your ears at the same time Takashi Inui's incredible shot reaches the net. Cheers and laughter here in your room, a thunder of stamped feet rolling across the ceiling from the main bar above.

"This is a surprise right?" asks one of the non-watchers, "Japan aren't better than Belgium?"

Jan Vertonghen's looping header causes a ripple of disappointment; Marouane Fellaini's equaliser brings sighs and a return to conversations that had lay dormant for twenty minutes. Gentle introductory chat with the boyfriend of a friend; piecing together how you all know each other, some of you once, twice, three times removed from the group that first set foot in this pub together. It was easier then, the recurring in-jokes about your coupledom; none of you ever expected they'd stop being relevant. Least of all you.

"Straight down his throat," says one of you with disappointment as a late Japanese corner is clutched by Thibaut Courtois. And in the time it takes you to glance at the clock and back to the action, Kevin De Bruyne is crossing halfway; Thomas Meunier on the overlap, a step-over from Romelu Lukaku, Nacer Chadli sweeps the ball home. There are screams and shrieks of delight from above your heads. Seven touches from end to end, a counter-attack as smooth as it was clinical. Ten seconds and done; the sort of fleeting moment of perfection you invest a lifetime of watching the game for. You could watch it over and over for hours.

But instead you're standing, supping up drinks, picking up bags, putting down glasses and pushing back chairs. Outside on the pavement, hugs, pats on the shoulder, waves. You all part ways and move off in different directions, and you cross the road to head back to London Bridge alone. You look at your phone; if you hurry you can make the 21.13, but why rush? Why any urgency for yet more emptiness?

Sweden 1-0 Switzerland

Day twenty-something of a UK heatwave. No-one can remember what a cloud looks like. Grass is now yellow unless stated otherwise. Pigeons and people dot around Waterloo Millennium Green. Smoke, reggae, and hammed up domestic arguments drift across the park from the jerk chicken stall beneath the trees. A big man in high-vis trousers is beached on a bank. By the Waterloo Road entrance, a child plays Scatch with his mum as if it's 1992; beyond the fence, opposite The Old Vic, buses stand idle, their drivers leaning against the railings in short-sleeves and conversation.

People eat from styrofoam boxes and paper bags. Between mouthfuls of rice and peas a woman on a bench laughs loudly through a hands-free phone call. The uniform of choice is stripped back office clothes, minimum layers, lanyards dancing in the breeze. A man shakes a picnic blanket, sending a cloud of dust and dead grass in the direction of others seated nearby. Clothes are dusted down, a bin overflows; intermittent yells and cheers and laughter carry from the six-a-side football court.

Back in the office for a 3pm meeting. Stray, unoccupied chairs pulled around a communal table too small for its current purpose. Shorts, linen shirts, light skirts, summer dresses, the hum of the air conditioning; blinds pulled down on another scorcher of a day. Over and done with, back to your desk; the sight of small red and yellow figures moving about the top corner of your Swedish colleague's screen. You ask her the score.

"It's nil-nil," she tells you. "It's all very even so far – quite neutral really." You suggest that may be playing into Switzerland's hands. The joke is lost in translation, you hope.

Someone has opened a window, the air conditioning can't compete and so you take this as a cue to retreat to the foyer of a different building, a place where not only will it be cooler, but you'll also be able to keep a keener eye on the match. Once there you watch Emil Fosberg's shot ricochet into the net via a Swiss boot as above your screen dignitaries are guided round the space; heads following the direction of arm gestures at recent refurbishments. At other tables people work freelance, taking advantage of the quiet and the WiFi, whilst pensioners in for a cuppa tut at the ratio of one person per table. A security guard stands by the door fiddling with his radio, small children patter in from the fountain outside; wet feet smacking against the marble floor.

Colombia 1-1 England

A steady stream of international students, each carrying identical shoulder bags, flow two-by-two in through the west entrance of Baker Street station. You stand to one side, allowing them to pass, impatiently wishing you hadn't; the end of their train never in sight. Next to you stands a woman looking quizzically at her phone, somehow dressed impeccably in all white despite the clammy heat of the city; a living, breathing detergent advert.

You head westwards towards Paddington. The streets are quiet save for the metronomic squeak of a shopping trolley being wheeled along the opposite pavement, its noise matching your stride. As you walk down Bell Street, the scene is being set in Moscow; through the doors of The Bell House you see the players standing in the tunnel of the Otkritie Arena. On a television in the Ahl Cairo Egyptian restaurant they are belting out the anthems as one of the proprietors stands outside the doors, smoking.

You duck into The Green Man, order an overpriced syrup-mix cola and nestle in a distant corner by the door to the upstairs hostel, a spot that offers you a view of about eighty percent of the screen and a light breeze from the window. On the table in front of you sit a couple of middle-class women enjoying their biannual bout of football partisanship. What they lack in awareness of the game, they trump in commitment, "Yes!" shouts one, enthusiastically applauding the decidedly regulation awarding of an England throw-in.

Though all others present are enraptured, you are not. The game is awful. Tedious, tactical, and devoid of genuine chances.

You're at least afforded a brief smile by Harry McGuire's desperate in-the-round miming of a video screen, done without ever truly knowing at whom he is supposed to direct such an appeal. The pub crowd grows as the half wears on – a trio of Americans from the hostel upstairs, a netball team flush from a nearby fixture – all squeezing into uncomfortable spaces, but ones that offer them a glimpse of Russia.

"Did he just push him? That can't be allowed," shouts the woman in front of you as you crunch your teeth together on your final ice-cube and pick your way apologetically between bodies to the door.

The streets are, unsurprisingly, quieter than on most Tuesdays. Even the usually snarling Edgware Road feels like a side-street. The population that would normally fill the grass of Merchant Square or the terraces of Paddington Basin on a sun-drenched evening such as this are instead contained behind glass; in bars and cafes, jostling together, sweating shoulder to sweating shoulder, drinks cradled against chests.

In another upstairs room on the corner of Little Venice you once again struggle to find the words to articulate the barrier of gloominess that seems to separate you from the world everyone else is living. You can feel tears again, creeping round the edges of your eyes, and your therapist encourages you to let them go and you want to and you don't all at the same time. Instead you stare over her shoulder, at the shadow of the balcony iron work edging slowly across the wallpaper with the setting sun; at a plane cutting across the blue rectangle of sky, at your own feet and at hers, as from somewhere outside the sound of a choir carries through the open window.

By the time you've descended back onto the towpath and wiped the moisture from your eyes, the game has edged into extra-time. But you're not ready for a crowd, and besides, the forty minutes you saw were tedious enough. So you choose to walk on, and take advantage of empty streets and quiet Tube lines, and the cooler dark evening air. You pass the excited crowds huddled together in The Chapel, all eyes fixed on distant corners of the bar, and people packed against the windows of The Globe. A chant of 'come on England' carries across the street as a man bedded down outside Baker Street station picks up another pizza crust from the box by his feet.

You reach London Bridge just as the penalties are about to begin, and with fifteen minutes until the next train home you step out of the station onto Tooley Street, where a huge crowd has gathered at the Shipwright Arms; as dense outside the pub as it is inside, fanning across to the opposite side of the road where people try to follow the drama between passing buses. The penalties commence and each one follows the same soundscape; loud murmurs and shouts, followed by a split second of silence, before a collective cheer or groan.

"Are you Colombian?" asks a young woman sat on a nearby wall as the screens in the bar show Mateus Uribe's spot-kick rebounding from the bar, this time in slow motion.

"Sorry?"

"You don't seem as excited as everyone else watching."

"Oh, no," you say. "I'm Welsh."

"That explains it," she says, with a smile.

And you don't know how to carry on the conversation, even though you'd very much like to. You hesitate in the hope some words will come forth, but nothing does, and you can feel your feet tensing in embarrassment, so you just smile awkwardly before turning back to look between the heads and the limbs on the pub's apron.

Kieran Trippier scores. A huge cheer. More people join the crowds on the pavement. Jordan Pickford saves from Carlos Bacca. An even bigger cheer. On the upper deck of a passing bus a young woman elbows her friend and points to the pub under siege below. Eric Dier steps up. The camera pans back. His foot meets the ball, and the ball meets the net and inside, through the glass, arms flail and fists are clenched and sprays of alcohol catch the green light of the big screen.

You turn and jog through the station entrance and up the stairs to platform one, just as a quintet of train station staff burst out of an office door in celebration. A chorus of 'It's Coming Home' drifts up from the street below as the train doors shut behind you. The night sky is purple; save for a thin orange band that hugs the horizon in the west, silhouetting city landmarks in your wake as you look out the window and lose count of the red lights of cranes that stretch out across the rest of the sky.

South Korea & Japan 2002

In a state of flux between Lincoln and Doncaster; a first year at university you'd had to abandon half-way through. Not ready. Spurred on only when you found the right course and realised what you were missing, and what you could have.

Lunchtime drinking in The Quayside that devolved into afternoons spent in beer gardens; watching Niki get so into her first ever World Cup match she was the most nervous person in the pub as the clock ran down on England-Argentina. Breakfast viewing in your mum's front room. A text of Goooooooooooooolllll!!! from Alan within seconds of Dario Rodriguez' spectacular volley hitting the back of the Danish net. Another England game; Nigeria watched with Jane – a school-friend who'd crashed in your sister's old room following a heavier than planned Thursday night reunion for the four of you who'd gone off to university. Sick in your kitchen sink, she was an assistant headteacher not long after the next tournament.

Working in the Miners' Welfare Club on the afternoon of the final. Leant on the bar, bored, watching a distant television perched on a shelf above the pool table, the same one you'd spent your childhood Saturday afternoons watching the classified results on. Then, here with your dad cradling a syrupy coke mix, when this place was full of sports teams and smoke and Stones Bitter ashtrays on formica table tops. Now, standing bar-side of a near empty room whilst a woman nudged her husband and asked "that Brazil goalkeeper, is he Swedish?"

The quarter finals

Uruguay 0-2 France

You booked this afternoon off weeks ago. Fresh out of time off in lieu or convenient excuses to be elsewhere, but wanting to ensure you saw the last of the tournament's office-hour kick-offs. But your forward planning, as with so much in your orbit, suffered from a lack of further motivation. And so, ten minutes before kick-off, you're here in Farringdon, plodding muggy streets without any clear sense of where you're going.

At the Holborn end of Leather Lane you give up on your own intuition and, leaning on a wall between office-break vapers, type the word 'pub' into your phone. As the map reloads you gaze up at the modernist chocolate box apartments of Vesage Court; no signs of life, just a couple of St. George's cross flags fluttering from balconies. You put your phone back in your pocket and, purely because it's all of forty yards away, you settle on The Argyle.

Very quickly you wish you hadn't. Like a first-day apprentice in a busy restaurant kitchen, wherever you stand you're in the way of someone or something. You resort to wedging yourself in behind a quiz machine with a view of the television screen that is practically side on. If that were the worst of it, it wouldn't be so bad. But then there's the rugby team reunion in the corner; their projected banter drowning out commentary the barman has just turned up to 100.

"Hey, do you reckon they have baguettes at half time? Phil? ...Phil! ...Do you reckon they have baguettes at half-time? ...The French? At half-time?"

"Aye aye, who's she? Did you see her in the crowd there?"

"Nah, everyone hates the French... aaah, just joking Marco, just joking. Your face!"

"Hawheehawheehawheehaw."

Fifteen minutes is all you can take. You put your glass on the bar and step out through the door.

You head down Greville Street where, lunchtime rush over, the staff of the falafel shop are wiping tables and carrying rubbish bags from the door to the kerbside. On Hatton Garden a van is being guided into a parking space, a woman holds her hand up to the sky to photograph a new ring; through a jewellers' window you see a young salesman following a couple round the store. Down the hill to Farringdon where builders sit and squat in the shade of Wetherspoon's facade, cigarettes and phones in hand, pints at their feet.

You take a one-stop hop on the Circle Line to shave some time from your walk, before stepping into the small pasta shop on Goswell Road. The solitary employee asks your order the moment you step in, causing you to panic purchase, and as he disappears into the kitchen you take a handful of napkins and wipe the sweat from your forehead and neck. Sam Matterface's voice carries from the kitchen, emanating from an old portable television perched on a high shelf between colanders. As you stand waiting for the man to re-emerge with your meal, France take the lead. You duck and swivel like a boxer avoiding punches to try and find a line of sight to the screen, between the pots, pans and utensils that hang from the shelves. Standing side on, bent backwards at the waist, chin to your shoulder, you are just about able to see Raphael Varane get across his man in slow motion to glance the ball goalwards.

Out the door, a heat haze rises from the tarmac as you cross into the Golden Lane Estate. A dashed cheer from the back room of The Shakespeare has two smokers turning abruptly to the pub windows to put their hands to the glass and peer in. You move on, find a seat in the half shade of the Roscoe Street flats, and eat quickly in an effort to be finished for the second half. As you rue the volume of capers in your order, two men sleep on the grass beneath the trees; the only noise the chatter from the outdoor tables at Fix Coffee, an occasional bird song, and the dulled chugs and thuds of a distant building site.

You step between smokers and in the door of The Trader just as the second-half is getting underway. A former colleague sits on a chair with his back to the bar and you head over to him, getting his updates on the chances you missed, before locating a similarly undersized seat and joining him properly. A trio of older men sit and don't speak around a nearby table, a barmaid pauses from her glass collection to fuss a dog; a man reverses a mobility scooter towards the door, Antoine Griezemann's shot goes through Fernando Muslera's hands and with half an hour left that's pretty much that.

Brazil 1-2 Belgium

Sweat drips from foreheads as you stand on the pavement outside the pub; bags between you, propped up against a bollard. The national flags that hung outside the pub a fortnight ago are gone; moved inside away from the wind, the birds, and vexillological souvenir hunters. To a man you hold a drink in each hand; a soft drink to aid the recovery from seven-a-side played in a searing heatwave and the subsequent sauna-like subterranean changing room, and a pint to aid the transition into evening.

Around you people stand in shorts, shades and loose light dresses; flesh pinking or bronzing beneath a sun yet to drop behind the towers of the Golden Lane and Peabody Estates; all of you hugged by an air thick with the sticky, dirty heat of a seemingly endless city heatwave.

As the clock ticks towards kick-off you move yourselves inside and pack around a table at the far end of the bar. Predictions and preferences are aired, the quality of Belgium's line-up and kit admired. An early corner bounces off Thiago Silva's thigh and grazes a post and you wonder why no-one else in the pub has noticed, until there's a collective "ooooh" some time after your own.

The television you're watching is around eight seconds ahead of the others in the pub. Collectively you take pleasure in frustrating other drinkers by exaggerating your reactions to events on the field, until a grinning barman spoils your fun, turning the screen off and off again. You've only just finished your theatrical booing as the ball flies into the Brazilian net. Quarter of an hour later Romelu Lukaku and Kevin De Bruyne's ruthless counter-attack has you applauding.

At full-time you all go your separate ways; waves with one hand, bags slung over shoulders with the other, the final sip of a pint sunk as you turn on your heels. Outside, two men in Belgium shirts are embracing and slapping each other on the back, watched by the smokers seated beneath the awning. Once again taxi cabs line the road south of Roscoe Street; the laughter of their owners carrying through the open upstairs windows of Kennedy's.

A man behind the counter of Barbican Pizza shuffles empty boxes as a Belgian player is interviewed on the screen behind him. The last of the post-work office drinkers stand in ever decreasing circles on the pavement outside the Two Brewers where empty glasses line the window-sills. In City Square people in headphones watch *Breakfast at Tiffany's* from rows of deckchairs, a woman nearby crouches in a doorway to rearrange her handbag; a couple embrace on a bench. You descend into the heat of Moorgate station.

Sweden 0-2 England

Nottingham. Another weekend escape from the city. This time for a football tournament. An eighteenth year out of nineteen; a schoolboy when you first pulled on the shirt, this year returning as a veteran.

On the University of Nottingham campus, the meadow grass of The Downs, at odds with its lush green depiction on the signs that mark it, crinkles and sways bright yellow in the light of another high summer sun. On the lake beneath the Portland Building families and friends drift idly in hire boats, too hot to move under their own power. People with ice-creams watch on from benches on the bank, and chat from behind sunglasses on the tables outside the Theatre Cafe.

Under the gaze of a dozen geese a man practices a personal and somewhat unique take on tai-chi in the shade of a tree. Laughter carries from the crazy golf course; a car turns uncertainly into a road, its two occupants gazing around from the open windows, looking for some kind of reassurance as to their route. A solitary bird flaps across the clear blue sky.

A tinny chorus of '*Football's Coming Home*' comes from an upstairs window in Rutland Hall as three lads in England shirts hurry across the courtyard with clinking carrier bags. In a darkened ground floor common room – blinds drawn to bring clarity to the big screen on a far wall – your teammates of ten years and more are dissecting their morning's endeavours; mocking poor touches, and wayward finishes whilst the Swedish anthem comes to a close above their heads.

Occasionally people you don't know stick their heads in the door, and, getting sight of the two recycling bins repurposed and filled with ice and cans – one bitter, one lager – shake their head at the ingenuity of your set-up. Some stay for a few minutes, some move on quickly. Half an hour in and Harry Maguire bullets a header into the Swedish net; everyone else in the room leaps out of their chairs and onto their feet. Hands in the air; clumsy high fives and fist pumps. You're the only one who remains seated, but you're happy, contented at witnessing collective joy on familiar faces.

Russia 2-2 Croatia

Your eyes open on an unfamiliar ceiling and you twist your body to face the rest of the room. How long were you asleep? You reach for your phone. It's 7.30pm. You've missed a third of the match, and also – as shown by the run of messages and missed calls – the departure of your teammates for the planned evening meal. You wonder whether it's worth it? You could just stay here; save an evening of awkward conversation shouted over loud music, feeling unease despite being surrounded by people you've known for so long. The expectation to be conversational, relaxed, fun. It paralyses you more than it ever should.

You force yourself into the shower and a clean set of clothes, out the door and across the campus, out onto Beeston High Street, glancing from side to side to try and spy the pub three of your team are holed up in. The Jesse Boot's unwelcoming exterior gives way to an equally unsettling interior; ferociously hot with a smell of stale smoke that's reminiscent of stepping outside a Slavic airport in high summer, it's a book well judged by its cover.

Thankfully you don't hang about, moving instead to the comparatively fresh air outside The Malt Shovel. You keep up with the match only through forays to the bar or to the toilets and instead entertain yourself by watching the death-defying exploits of a kitten on an upstairs window ledge. The rest of the team joins you and you spill over a couple of tables; two or three conversations carrying at once; a constant laughter track. You can't understand why you were ever worried.

A shout of "Penalties!" from the doorway empties the outdoor tables and people hurry inside to find a vantage point around the solitary television. You stay outside, convinced by a teammate's insistence he can stream it via his phone. A quartet of heads crowd over the tiny screen that stops and starts through a couple of spot-kicks before you give up and head inside, to discover reality is three penalties ahead of you. As

Croatian players run and dive and slide into a pile, to the despair of a watching stadium, taxis are ordered, 'drink up' is mimed, and the night continues on.

Germany 2006

Settled in Lincoln now. The final throes of a Students' Union role and matches watched with anyone who'd hung around for the onset of summer. Cheering on a Germany-Costa Rica goal-fest with Sam, watching Argentina slide through Serbia & Montenegro with Dave.

In the early stages of a relationship begun on the down low, her a keen football fan, meant England games watched in pubs you otherwise rarely visited. Standing by the doors in The Glasshouse as Peter Crouch pulled Brent Sancho's hair to nod in a goal against Trinidad & Tobago on a screen above the bar. Being the one person stood still as The Square Sail erupted around you to Joe Cole's volley against Sweden. Packed sofas for Argentina-Mexico; a housewarming for that place with the terrible carpet the three of you had just moved into on Blenheim Road.

Boarding a plane for the United States the day after England's exit; the unsettling feeling of strapping into your first long-haul flight whilst the person across the aisle read a newspaper headlined 'End of the World'. Germany playing Italy in the background of a Dallas bar where you drank unnecessarily strong porter as you caught up with Charlotte and met her partner who you didn't much care for. Seeing your by then not-so-secret girlfriend off as she climbed into an airport bound taxi in the early hours of a San Antonio morning; your trip adjusted to cross paths. And later that day,

Italy and France playing out the final on an ancient hotel television; the Spanish commentary almost drowned out by air conditioning cranked up to full-blast to combat the fierce Texan heat.

The semi finals

France 1-0 Belgium

Evening shadows are edging along Praed Street; a net curtain flaps out of an open window. An ambulance siren makes you jump. A pair of businessmen lower their sunglasses to watch a woman half their age walk by. A middle-aged man staring at his phone screen trips over a kerb and tries to style it out, a young man on a hire-bike waves to a group of friends at a cafe table.

You take a seat on a Paddington Basin pontoon and open up another supermarket sandwich. A trio of young lads try to lure weary security staff into a chase by mounting a nearby barge. Families picnic and play on the pavement outside restaurants; tanned, blonde women in gym gear stride confidently past outdoor tables. The sunlight reflects off the office blocks and dapples on the water where a duckling picks up the pace to try and catch its mother and five siblings; two geese are photographed by a man in a suit. The pontoon shakes to the eager dance-steps of a girl in pigtails and school uniform who implores her mum to look up from her phone. A man in a France shirt walks by carrying a tall upright office fan.

You're back in the same pub at the end of the water. Back nursing another soft drink at a table by the window, only this time there are more heads to look above, more people asking if they can take nearby stools. The noise that greets a brilliant Hugo Lloris save brings the people at the outdoor tables, and those just passing by, rushing to the windows to see what has caused the excitement. On forty minutes you tip the last of the ice-cubes into your mouth, pick up your bag and move for the door. As you head towards Little Venice, Alan Shearer's punditry follows you down the towpath, from the bars and barges along the water.

Back in another two-chaired room, clock ticking on the table. This time not facing the water, but on the other side, somewhere above The Westway. The noise of the traffic carrying through the open window, the occasional wail of a siren, the beep of a horn, and a man's voice shouting "They all know now... they all know now anyway." In here, however, there is only silence. Your therapist, patient as ever whilst you stare fixedly at the floor, at her shoes, at the pattern of her rucksack propped up against her chair.

The seconds and the minutes continue to tick-tock by, but still all else is silent. You can't speak, can't articulate, can't voice why it is you remain so low, so flat, so empty. Your toes curl in your trainers in frustration at your inability to speak out to a person full of empathy and understanding, a person who holds no judgement, a person who just wants to help. Who you want to help. But you can't help yourself, so what hope have either of you got? Especially when all you can do is sit and stare at the floor and fail to find words, not so much as an adjective on which you can try to hang the cloak you've covered yourself in.

Croatia 2-1 England

On Leyton Road men in sandals and shalwar kameez stroll to the mosque in twos, past a trio of barbers sitting idle in their shop; one in the chair, two in the window. A young lad in football boots clops past you, jogging towards the pitches at Drapers Field, where a junior team training session is already underway. At the traffic lights a man rests his elbow through his open window whilst speaking loudly into a carphone in a language you can't identify. An England flag flaps from a van heading in the other direction.

There's an air of expectation, of everyone needing to be somewhere else. Shutters are coming down over shop fronts, cars swerve rather than turn into side roads, people in the windows of buses are glancing at watches. In The Leyton Star, a group of people are already in position beneath a television screen, 90 minutes ahead of time. A man with an England flag cape carries a crate of beer down from the flyover. In Best Fried Chicken two men are trying to fix a table and chairs; the whole connected furniture five-piece upturned in the middle of the shop, tools clanking off the tiled floor, whilst customers eat around them.

You pick up a couple of cans from the artisan deli turned cafe-bar on Francis Road, where people in shorts and sun-hats are already sitting in the backyard around a sun-washed television screen. People hurry away from bus stops on the High Road and chance a crossing through the traffic; behind them the cricket field is as bereft of people as it is grass. You buzz what you hope is the right flat, send a text message for good measure, and eventually your friend comes to the door.

"There's a bit of a delay on it, because it's through the console," your friend had explained, going on to tell you how at the culmination of the England-Colombia game he had received text messages about the outcome before he'd finished watching it unfold. Now, as he stands outside the patio doors having an

115

early match cigarette, a disjointed burst of cheers and shouts echo around the block. He looks back in at you through the glass and holds his palms out open to the side, before moving to the open door.

"It's not is it?"

"Well, England have a free-kick," you reply and he holds what's left of his cigarette at arm's length behind him as he leans in through the doorway to watch Kieran Trippier take three quick steps up to the ball and send it flying over the wall, the defenders' heads craning quickly round to watch it hit the net.

"Bloody hell, it is" and he punches the air with his smoke-free hand, before retreating back outside for a celebratory puff.

His wife returns from an extended wait in a chip shop queue and three of you squeeze onto the sofa – you with a brightly coloured can, they with plates on their laps – in time to see Harry Kane unfathomably fail to extend England's lead. Groans and shouts again carrying through the open patio door from other flats in the block, before you've seen their source; effect and then cause.

When the ball is in midfield there's conversation, but despite their very clear hospitality and genuine warmth, you can never shake the feeling of being a third wheel. The body on the end of the sofa, the one not invested or involved in the outcome of the match; the gatecrasher. In the way, when you're clearly not, otherwise why would you have been invited? Were you always so self-aware? So short of confidence? Did you always feel as if you were such a burden, rather than an active participant?

By the time Croatia edge ahead in extra-time, the patio door has been closed to save you from spoilers. The Croatian players peel away to the corner flag where they tumble and fall onto photographers in abject glee, bringing you a smile that you feel obliged to hide. "The one moment they switched off," you offer over the replays, in an attempt to offer something in the way of impartial comment that won't frustrate or annoy.

Full-time in a quiet and sombre space; you feel out of place and lacking emotional involvement, as if you've accompanied a new spouse to the funeral of their distant relative. You offer condolences, because you like these people and you want them to be happy, but ultimately you have no equivocal experience. Whenever your own nation has fallen at the final hurdle you've been there, surrounded by people you know are feeling the same feelings with the same sincerity. You don't want to outstay your welcome and upset the solemnity with a misjudged comment. So you say a slow goodbye, a genuine thanks for the company, which is at least noticeably more sincere than your commiserations, and close the door behind you.

The sun has set by the time you walk back across Leyton, the air cooler, but not cold, the streets bereft of the urgency they had pre-match. Outside a late night mini-market on Francis Road a dog is fussed in the three languages; there's the noise of bottles going into a recycling bin from behind a side gate, the sound of dishes being washed from an open window. An angry man in an England shirt slaps a street sign in frustration, a woman in an 'It's coming home' t-shirt waits for the bus, home.

On Leyton High Road there are sombre queues inside takeaways; 'Kane 9' is slumped across a chicken shop counter, a trio of England shirts are failing to muster conversation in a kebab shop window. A quartet of England car flags lay discarded on the pavement, a couple console one another on the steps to T.K. Maxx. As you sit on the westbound platform at

Leyton station, eastbound Tubes arrive packed with replica shirts and disappointment; a solemn pair of eyes stare out at you from behind St. George's flag face paint.

South Africa 2010

Midway through a two-year stint in Worcester that you never truly made enough effort to settle into. You'd taken a job to be closer to an unrequited love, and never really found a purpose beyond that. Come the summer, a year of working fourteen hour Wednesdays had left you with enough time off in lieu to work only mornings in June. People thought you were living the dream.

Every single game but one watched in your sparsely furnished flat; the noise of the dual carriageway beneath carrying through windows left open to embrace a summer that was passing you by. You blogged and tweeted every game to feel connected, but in truth watched every single one alone. Skipped a big social outing with work to appear on the BBC World Service; booked to give an alternate view, but left hanging on a phone-line unable to interject. They didn't ask again.

The final was the only game you didn't watch in that flat – your contract having expired. No new place secured; you'd been forced to beg the university for temporary digs. You moved during the day – thirteen trips back and forth on foot, heckled as you carried an ironing board past the pubs on New Street – and watched the final in a student room; belongings piled up around you in boxes and bags as Howard Webb dished out card upon card, and you tried to work out what the hell you'd do next.

The third place play-off

Belgium 2-0 England

The smell of bonfire smoke drifts through the open window; the thwack of tennis balls on the television punctuated by Andrew Castle's daytime blandness. Outside, cyclists shout conversation as they speed past; someone is sawing some wood. You pull the front door shut behind you and step into the street where a woman is taking her Nissan Micra through a seven point turn; over the road a conversation is taking place across a hedge, and children, hair wet from the swimming baths down the road, are dawdling along the pavement behind parents.

On the train into Central London a quartet of lads are chatting loudly; leaving no-one in any doubt that they are most certainly lads, and most certainly 'on it'. In between the hiss of opening lager cans, they loudly project their banter down the carriage, keen to amplify the good time they're having. They depart at London Bridge in a cloud of aftershave and flurry of nudges, winks and nods towards an attractive young woman standing further down the aisle.

The City is relaxing in the quiet of a summer Saturday. Cheapside is almost pedestrian; on Gresham Street a banksman opposite a construction site dutifully holds a Stop/Go sign in the road, despite the superfluousness of each command. The slap of flip-flops and sandals on pavement would be the only sound were it not for the peeling bells of St. Lawrence Jewry. In an open door of the church two women in fascinators hold an earnest conversation. A small group of tourists are guided to look up at The Guildhall, whilst a priest emerges from another door; he rounds the corner – to where bridesmaids and pageboys skip around the small ornate pond – reaches into his top pocket, and pulls out a pipe.

Beyond a silent and empty Little Britain, past St. Bartholomew's Hospital and a faded World Cup wallchart pinned up in the dust cloaked window of Beppe's Cafe. You pass through the Grand Avenue of Smithfield Market, sunshine through its upper windows casting a barcode of light and shadow across the railings. As with the City, the streets of Farringdon are also a silent tribute to their weekday selves, just the sound of a solitary runner on Britton Street and two dog owners in conversation in St. John's Gardens.

You're heading to The Dovetail, a Belgian bar tucked down a passageway, but as you near it your confidence departs you once again. You glance at the door but just keep walking. The bar isn't packed but suddenly you're doubting your plans and your convictions. This anxiety has come in waves in the past few months, a sudden fear of being anywhere where you don't know anyone, where you worry people will judge you for being on your own. You know it's nonsense. That it's just a pub and that no-one will care, but that doesn't stop you from being where you find yourself now, standing in the shade of Clerkenwell Green, pretending to look at your phone whilst you try to summon the confidence to go back.

Fifteen minutes it takes before you finally convince yourself to return, to step inside, by which time you've already missed out, both on Belgium's opening goal and any seats within a reasonable vantage point of the projector screen. You choose a beer that takes your mind back to the comforting surrounds of

Lille two summers back, and perch yourself near the door on a stool that just about offers a view of the match.

A couple passing through the alley pause in the doorway behind you.

"It's one-nil already," says the man.

"Who's playing?" asks his female companion.

"Belgium and England."

"Belgium and who?"

"England."

"But England are out, we watched it."

"No it's the third place match."

"Oh Belgium are leading? That's a bit shit."

"Yeah no-one cares about this match anyway."

"Yeah."

And on they go, national fervour dissolved in only a handful of days.

England continue to huff and puff whilst you – taking advantage of vacated seats and tables – steadily edge your way nearer to the screen. Eric Dier suddenly channels the spirit of Archie Gemmill '78 and skips through the Belgian defence before chipping the ball over Thibaut Courtois, but just as arms go into the air from the tables either side of you, Toby Alderweireld appears out of nowhere to hook the ball into the stand.

"What's it going to take? Seriously?" barks a rotund middle-aged man who's spent the game working his way through the bar's cocktail menu with his much younger, and now much sleepier, female companion.

Into the final ten minutes and Eden Hazard gets in behind Phil Jones to slot the ball into the bottom corner and double Belgium's lead. A dozen people in the corner of the bar, clad invariably in Belgian flag face-paint and Belgium shirts, rise to their feet cheering, clinking glasses in celebration.

"Why are they still trying?" asks a woman of her friends as England restart the match.

"Harry Kane might get the golden boot," one replies.

She pauses to look at the screen for a while before replying, "I don't know what that is."

The final

France 4-2 Croatia

London is baking. The heatwave that has engulfed the city now seemingly eternal; sky the bright, fresh blue of a child's painting, clouds as infrequent as a rural bus service. Granary Square is packed to the edges, a barely moving sea of sunglasses and bare skin; children run through the fountains, people picnic on the pavements. The amphitheatre steps that run down to the canal are thick with bodies, and the smells of suncream and alcohol; the laconic sound of tennis, broadcast on the big screen, juxtaposing with chatter, laughter and the beat of dance music from portable speakers.

You pick your way between outstretched limbs and melting ice-cubes down the steps to the towpath, where reddening bodies lay out on narrowboat roofs, and a tired child is carried by a weary parent. A cooling breeze from the water cascading over St. Pancras lock offers brief respite from the heat as a Eurostar clatters overhead. Cycle bells tinkle and kids are corralled aside. A moorhen bobs along the surprisingly clear water, dogs pant happily down the pavement, graffiti shows its brightest colours. The serenity only briefly punctuated as a cyclist glides past with the sounds of MC Hammer emanating from his backpack. You can't touch this.

Only as you get into Camden are there signs of the World Cup Final's imminency; a trio of red and white checkered shirts disappearing into Camden Town Underground station, two men draped in tricolours on the junction of Parkway and Arlington Road. You pause at a coffee shop to buy something icy, and to grab a handful of napkins with which to mop your brow, before awaiting the descent of your friend and his French girlfriend to the door that leads to their flat.

Back down the hill to the High Street. The bars are starting to fill up, a slight buzz of anticipation. You pack into the corner of your fourth choice pub, the first one at which your friend's girlfriend was successful in reserving a table. You hate the practice, but you're glad she did it. The beer is disappointing, but at least you have a table to put it down on, sight of a television screen, and an aspect of shade from the flags of competing nations hung over the windows. And though much of this group in which you find yourself are not regular football fans, they are at least French enough to hold a vested interest.

The music that has boomed out of speakers since you stepped through the door is cut, the players emerge, and the sound of the National Anthems fills the space. Unable to determine one group of attractive European twenty-somethings from another you scan the room to see who joins in with which song – turns out you'd wrongly attributed a good quarter of the pub's nationality. A woman by the bar takes off her glasses before lifting her jumper over her head to unveil a Hrvatska t-shirt, and as she repositions her spectacles and brushes her hair back behind her ears and laughs at one of her companions you realise you're staring rather than glancing and your friend was trying to pass you a menu and the match kicked off minutes ago.

You'd expected a huge cheer when France took the lead, but the reality – from your corner of the pub at least – was much more subdued. A brief moment of arms in the air before applause. A reaction more befitting of a hold of serve in a second round match at Wimbledon than the opening goal in the biggest football fixture on the planet. The Croatian equaliser brings a more vociferous cheer, leaps in the air and table-wide hugs and high fives; why couldn't your friend's girlfriend have been from Lika-Senj rather than Lyon? Such is the stare he gets when joining you in complementing the crispness of Ivan Perisic's strike there's a chance he briefly entertains the same thought.

The giant Argentinian referee makes the signal for a VAR review and the pub makes the sort of noise you'd ordinarily hear when a couple on a quiz show elect to gamble for the star prize. Light chatter, questions asked, answers debated, the referee turns and runs back onto the grass; draws another square in the air and points to the spot. There are cheers, shouts of protestation, shakes of the head, but it's 2-1 at half-time and the friend you'd talked out of betting on a high-scoring final is as unimpressed as the Croat clientele.

The second-half brings more goals. The Croatian goalkeeper's dives, the sort that are kindly described as 'despairing' by commentators; as if he'd turned up expecting a narrower goal frame. "What was he doing?" shouts a nearby drinker as Hugo Lloris takes it on himself to make matters more interesting, but the game is as good as won, and the quintet of French lads nearby know it. As the clock ticks down, they unpin the tricolour from the pub's ceiling, and hug and huddle together; slapping backs and bouncing on their toes. When the final whistle goes, they leap around ecstatically, one of them landing on your ankle, your yelp of pain not registering as they jump up and down some more, before tumbling out the door and into the street.

From beyond the windows you hear a chanted Marseillaise and the beeping of car horns. You finish your drink and say your goodbyes – handshakes, waves and a kiss on each cheek – before stepping out into the comparatively fresh warmth of Camden High Street. There's a warm yellow glow to the sky, the evening light dappling through the trees of the alleyway opposite. The French lads from the pub are waving their flag and their fists at passing motorists. You look up and down the road; the diversion is over and done with, where do you go from here?

The days after

There is no longer bunting in the barber shop windows; the flag of Portugal no longer flaps in that Elmira Street garden. Fixtures have been wiped from chalkboards that once again promise beer gardens and free WiFi. There are no more white spaces on the office wallchart, no more desktop windows on Russia, the colleague whose monitor had a French flag taped to it this past month has swept £32 into their purse.

But the sun still shines. The grass is still yellow. Sleeves are still rolled up. Legs still bare. The landscape of London continues to be reflected back at you via the sunglasses of other people passing you by. Outdoor tables still fill with evening drinkers. The flat is still empty, the bed still hard to leave, the willingness to communicate still buried deep within.

"So," says your therapist as you look forlornly through the window, beyond the shadows of the balcony balustrades to another reddening sky; the sun once again dropping behind the high-rises, church spires and cranes of the scorching city. "We're out of time this week, but next time we'll talk about how you feel that it's all the good in your life that's died and only the shit remains."

Brazil 2014

London. In your thirties. A year into a relationship, a few months into a job you took great pride in. The hitherto unmet Chief Executive emerging from his office demanding to know where you were. Face draining until you realised he just wanted in on the sweepstake you'd set up. He pulled out Switzerland. "At least the flag's a big plus," you'd said, but got nothing back.

A city awash with flags. Not just England, but Algeria, Greece, Colombia, Portugal, Argentina. Hanging from shop awnings and balconies, cafe windows and newsagents. On a roof in Hoxton for a party of people you hardly knew; crowded round a phone screen to watch Dutch goals rain on Spain. Gary beckoning you behind his reception desk to see Tim Cahill's wonder goal against the Netherlands. Passing a restaurant in Clapham and being startled by the huge cheer from an upstairs window that told you Algeria had scored. Lying together on Clapham Common as a friend arrived with news of a Portugal goal.

You watched matches around the city; James Rodriguez' volley bringing The Lost Hour to its feet, Balham Bowls Club cheering Germany's sixth goal and then erupting in laughter as the camera panned to tearful Brazilian fans. Watching Costa Rica's final throes in The Yacht, a pint on your own in Farringdon for France against South Africa. You and George in that dull basement living room, doubled over laughing at Jonathan Pearce's failure to grasp goal-line technology. Dotted around a London Bridge boozer with your old university football team for the third place play-off.

Maybe that's why you had such high hopes for this tournament. Because the last one had come at a time of such positivity; had helped you to develop your attachment to a city you'd always had your doubts about. Just after the tournament you had met up with an old colleague for an hour or so. Sitting on the grass in one of the squares in Bloomsbury, she said you looked really well, that you looked really happy, and that it was good to finally see that.